Dan,

I got this for you as a gift because I thought it would speak to you as a musical artist and believer.

Love,

Dad

SCRIBBLING in the SAND

Christ

and

Creativity

Michael Card

InterVarsity Press
Downers Grove, Illinois
Leicester, England

InterVarsity Press, U.S.A.
P.O. Box 1400, Downers Grove, IL 60515-1426
World Wide Web: www.ivpress.com
E-mail: mail@ivpress.com

Inter-Varsity Press, England
38 De Montfort Street
Leicester LE1 7GP, England
World Wide Web: www.ivpbooks.com
E-mail: ivp@uccf.org.uk

InterVarsity Press® is the book-publishing division of InterVarsity Christian Fellowship/USA®, a
student movement active on campus at hundreds of universities, colleges and schools of nursing in the
United States of America, and a member movement of the International Fellowship of Evangelical
Students. For information about local and regional activities, write Public Relations Dept.,
InterVarsity Christian Fellowship/USA, 6400 Schroeder Rd., P.O. Box 7895, Madison, WI
53707-7895, or visit the IVCF website at <www.ivcf.org>.

Inter-Varsity Press, England, is the book-publishing division of the Universities and Colleges
Christian Fellowship (formerly the Inter-Varsity Fellowship), a student movement linking Christian
Unions in universities and colleges throughout the United Kingdom and the Republic of Ireland,
and a member movement of the International Fellowship of Evangelical Students. For information
about local and national activities write to UCCF, 38 De Montfort Street, Leicester LE1 7GP.

Cover design and illustration: Kirk DouPonce, UDG\DesignWorks

U.S. ISBN 0-8308-2317-4
U.K. ISBN 0-85111-985-9

Printed in the United States of America ∞

Library of Congress Cataloging-in-Publication Data

Card, Michael, 1957-
    Scribbling in the sand: Christ & creativity / Michael Card.
      p. cm.
    ISBN 0-8308-2317-4
    1. Creative ability—Religious aspects—Christianity. 2. Christian life. I. Title.
BT709.5 .C37 2002
233'.5—dc21
                                                                                2002023277

British Library Cataloguing in Publication Data
A catalogue record for this book is available from the British Library.

P	17	16	15	14	13	12	11	10	9	8	7	6	5	4	3	2	1
Y	14	13	12	11	10	09	08	07	06	05	04	03	02				

This book is dedicated to two people.

The first is someone who for twenty years I have heard say, "I'm not really creative." Susan, much of the burden for writing this book was to hopefully and finally convince you otherwise. You embody the truest, most Christlike form of creativity, the ability to seek and find and touch a person's heart.

The other person is my good friend Scott Roley, someone who by the world's standards is dazzlingly creative. A wonderful singer, songwriter, instrumentalist. Handsome and debonair to boot! Scott, you left all that behind because you heard and faithfully responded to the costly call to go deeper, to touch fewer people but in an infinitely more profound way. This book was written in gratitude for your sacrifice.

Contents

FOREWORD

━━━⟨∞⟩━━━

*C*hrist entered our world, the Creator translating heavenly existence to earthly. When our faith in Christ is combined with our own human efforts at creation, the act forges a richer and more diverse form of communication. Artists throughout the centuries have sought to tap into the transcendent by their creating. The language of the arts, it can be argued, is a language born of faith.

In other words, all art forms attempt to translate what is unseen into what is seen. Painter Joel Sheesley states, "I . . . suggest that the definition of content in art is very much like that New Testament definition of faith that calls faith 'the substance of things hoped for.'" Art, especially as we engage in it with a redeemed vision, becomes an activity of faith, translating the "substance of things hoped for" with words, paint and other materials into the content and form of art. Diversity is, then, created not out of deconstruction or fragmentation, but out of unity. Faith prompts us to create with a renewed language, uniting even the splintered language of the age and thus redeeming communication itself.

It is our desire that not just artists but the whole church be involved in this translation act. Ray Bakke writes, "The frontier of the world mission is no longer geographically distant; it's culturally distant but geographically right next door." This "distance" of culture exists not only in ethnic cultures but also in created new cultures in the city. The gap that exists between the culture at large and the church must be bridged by the gospel of incarnation, the "greatest translation."

Michael Card is a great storyteller. His music and his writings whisper into my soul the secret treasures of the gospel. His skill as a musician, and the depth of his thoughts, give a magical quality to his expression; through his work we enter an enchanted place, listening to a wise voice tell a wonderful old tale.

Many years ago in Japan, when I found my heart being renewed by Christ's presence in my life, a friend of mine suggested that I listen to Michael Card's songs. "Unfortunately," my missionary friend confided, "there aren't too many contemporary Christian musicians I can recommend to you" (he knew me well). "But Michael Card is different. You will appreciate him." My friend understood my struggles as an artist drawn by Christ but not having many examples of contemporaries leading in the arts.

It took me several years to hear Michael in person. When finally, one day in New Jersey, I listened to him perform, I had a strange sense of kinship. "The call is to community, the impoverished power that sets the soul free . . ." This prayer for community I made my own. I would be involved in the years to come, and up to this day, in a church planting movement in New York City, and would live out my calling as an artist there as director of the International Arts Movement (IAM).

As I now read through the manuscript of this book, I am so thankful to be involved with Michael once more in understanding creativity in the church and in the world. His words are deeply woven into the fabric of creativity, and into the struggle of asking God to create that community around him. While deeply rooted in ancient faith, his wisdom speaks to today's problems and the challenges we face in the church. Now, as our nation and our cities face darkness head on, his words move us even deeper into the mysteries of life and death. His poetry *(poiema)* encourages us all to be engaged in the creative act of expanding God's kingdom through the darkness. Michael leads us to see ourselves as God's masterpieces, created in Christ Jesus to create, in turn, masterpieces for God's glory.

—Makoto Fujimura
New York City

ACKNOWLEDGMENTS

———◦◦◦———

*M*ost of what is helpful about this book was born in community. It was called forth by the genuine needs of the community. The basic biblical concepts were born out of one of the first real communities of faith to which I ever belonged, a small biracial church in Bowling Green, Kentucky, called Cecelia Memorial Church. Here I first entered into a discipling relationship with Dr. William Lane, who has since gone home to be with Jesus. In many ways this book is only a continuation of his work. The concept of the creative mandate, the insights on the structure of the hymn fragment from Philippians, as a matter of fact almost every section of this book is based on a concept he taught me.

Several more of the ideas on devotional life and community were developed in a special community at Columbia International University where for four summers I taught a class called "Christ and the Creative Process." That class would not have been possible were it not for the support of Dr. David Osterland. It was he who first had the vision for the class. The content of this book was brought to maturity in the context of that class with his encouragement. Those students taught me more about the subject than I ever taught them.

I thank my covenant community here in Franklin, Tennessee: Scott Roley, who has walked with me for years in unqualified support and tears; Mike Smith and Dr. George Grant, who are currently pouring their lives into mine in the context of The Franklin House Discipleship Study Center. To the brothers of the larger covenant group, the Empty Hands Fellowship, I give thanks for your prayers. In more recent years Ken Cope, a brother who has come alongside my wife, Susan, and me, has opened the door of the human heart to us as no one else ever has. His teaching that we are not our gifts is a key to this discussion. Thanks to Ken also for working through this manuscript and forcing me to share from my own experience as "an act of repentance" for all the years of false humility.

Finally, I must thank Susan and our little community at home. She knows all too well the painful process of writing books, having written two of her own, and she helps free me up so I can write. She listens endlessly to ideas and false starts. She remains to me both a reminder of reality and the maker of dreams come true.

Chapter One

SCRIBBLING IN THE SAND

*I*t was art and it was theater at the same time, but it was more. It was what he did not say that spoke most powerfully to the mob that morning. It was a cup of cold water for a thirsty adulteress and an ice-cold drenching in the face to a group of angry Pharisees.

To this day we have not the slightest idea what it was Jesus twice scribbled in the sand. By and large the commentaries have asked the wrong question through the ages. They labor over the content, over what he might have written. They ask *what* without ever realizing that the real question is *why*. It was not the content that mattered but why he did it. Unexpected. Irritating. Creative.

They were furious, of course—as much with Jesus as with the woman. (For all we know, they may have set her up to be caught.) They dragged her into the temple court, interrupting who knows what luminous lesson Jesus was in the middle of.

You know the story. "What do you say?" they asked him, with

the false adoration he had become used to over time.

But he didn't say anything. Not a syllable. Instead Jesus crouched on his haunches and "wrote down" (*kata,* "down," *graphein,* "to write") something with his finger in the sacred sand of the temple.

The scribes and Pharisees could not bear his thoughtful silence and so kept prodding him with questions.

Finally Jesus broke the awful silence. Standing straight up once more, leaving his scribbling, he spoke, giving in ten simple words a summary of the wisdom and compassion that gave the perfect shape to his life (and can do the same to ours). "Whoever is without sin, let him cast the first stone."

Then he was at it again. The One who had traced the galaxies with that same finger, hunched over like a schoolboy, his tongue perhaps protruding from the corner of his mouth, writing once more those words we would give a treasure to know but never will.

A SPACE IN TIME

What Jesus did that morning created a space in time that allowed the angry mob first to cool down, then to hear his word, and finally to think about it, be convicted by it and respond—or not. It made time stand still. It was original. It was unexpected. It was a response to the noise and confusion and busyness all around him, yet it was not in the least tainted by the noise. Instead, Jesus' action created a frame around the silence—the kind of silence in which God speaks to the heart. In short, it was a supreme act of creativity. It was art.

The form and even the content apparently are not what

mattered, not as much as the fact that, for one moment, the noise stopped and the attention was focused elsewhere. And in that moment everyone around learned that their world was not the only world that existed. And so they were liberated. And that, too, is art.

Our encyclopedic books, our magnificent paintings, our grand symphonies, all the art ever done in his name since that day cannot hope to be more, and should not be allowed to be less, than Jesus' scribbling that morning in the sand. If what we create, write, dance or sing can open up such a space in time through which God may speak, imagine the possibilities! Painting might become a window through which a confused world looks and sees the sane order of God's creation. Music could become an orchestrated echo of the Voice the tired ears of humankind have longed for ages to hear. This is art through which God is seen and heard, in which he is incarnate, is "fleshed out" in paint and ink, in stone, in creative movement. From the flat, gray point of view of the fallen world they are only scratches and scribbles in the sand, but in the light of eternity they become the occasion for divine revelation. What more could we ever hope for, and once we've seen this new possibility, how could we ever settle for less?

∝∞∝

Scribbling in the Sand

Amidst a mob of madmen, she stood frightened and alone

As hate-filled voices hissed at Him that she should now be stoned

But in the air around Him hung a vast and wordless love

Who knows what luminous lesson He was in the middle of

At first He faced the fury of their self-righteous scorn

But then He stooped and at once became the calm eye of the storm

It was His wordless answer to their dark and cruel demand

A lifetime in a moment, as He scribbled in the sand

It was silence. It was music

It was art. It was absurd

He stooped and shouted volumes

Without saying a single word

The same finger of the strong hand

That had written ten commands

For now was simply scribbling in the sand

Within the space of space and time He'd scribbled in the sand

They came to hear and see as much as they could understand

Now bound by cords of kindness they couldn't cast a single stone

And Jesus and the woman found that they were all alone

Could that same Finger come and trace my soul's sacred sand

And make some unexpected space where I could understand

That my own condemnation pierced and broke that gentle Hand

That scratched the words I'll never know

Written in the sand

Tall and clear-eyed, Jennifer stepped into my borrowed office. "Can I ask you a question?" she asked. "I really wanted to take your class on creativity, but I read in the syllabus that we'll be required to make a class presentation."

"Yes," I said. "It's the most wonderful time we will have in class."

At this I noticed her hands nervously beginning to shake. I later learned that Jennifer had taken private cello lessons for years yet had never once performed for an audience. She was too afraid, she said: "Stage fright."

In the weeks that followed, together with perhaps twenty other students, we worked through the life of the Jesus she so dearly loved and longed to please. We looked at his life, his creativity. We strained to listen to his call on each of our lives, to see and feel the shape of it. It was about him, not aesthetics, not philosophy, not theory.

When the final class project night came, she waited until almost the last to give her presentation, a solo cello piece. I was nervous for her as she took her place before the class. I admired her courage. Responding to God's call sometimes means doing the last thing in the world we want to do. But she was doing this no longer for herself, but for him.

The music was glorious. She was lost in the process and so were we. It was a wordless time of worship for the class. It was a space in time. There were tears in her eyes and mine. She had not learned a lot of facts or information. She had spent time gazing into the face of Creativity itself. She had become lost in the process . . . and found. She is now the first chair in the cello section of her local symphony— perhaps often no less fearful, but undoubtedly aware of the call of God on her life.

I put Jennifer's story here because what happened in her heart and life I pray might happen in yours and mine. This is the best way I know of explaining what this book is about—to tell you stories.

LIFE IS A STORY

This book is not a synthesis of the ideas of others. That was what I wanted it to be at first. I had spent much time reading through the literature on creativity and the imagination, primarily focusing on the thoughtful writings of Calvin Seerveld and my dear friend Harold Best. These faithful brothers represent a lifetime of pondering the issues involved. As I read them, a sense of continuous gratitude overflowed in me for all their creative efforts. I had hoped to synthesize their major themes into one grandiose vision of my own.

After some months of frustrated effort, by grace I realized that to write such a book was not only beyond my abilities, it was not what I was being called to do. Thanks be to God that that realization came when it did.

Neither is this book a "how-to," "cheer you on to creativity" type of book. Many of the secular books on the topic are just that—full of techniques, some of which are truly helpful, many of which are a complete waste of time. But I cannot reduce this mystery into a few simple steps. There are some truths around the boundary of it that we can know, but the depths are beyond us. We can meditate on it and pray about it but never dissect, systematize or synthesize it. This is the vision I want to share with you, a Christ-centered vision of the creative process as a road to him.

This project has weighed heavily on my heart for some years now. I've wasted much time complaining about the lack of both faith and creativity in the industrial world of contemporary religious music. Yet I have contributed little to the discussion but my own negativity. So in one sense this book is sort of an apology, and it is an attempt to focus the discussion on Christ. What I have to offer, indeed all any Christian has to offer, is a window into the weakness of my own frustrated efforts.

So that is what I purpose to do: share with you, out of the tremendous wealth of my fragileness and brokenness, the story of how Jesus Christ met me, walked with me, strengthened me and gave me new songs to sing! At the cul-de-sac of my counterfeit eloquence I encountered true and profound beauty in the humility, servanthood and radical obedience of Jesus, the One I repeatedly confront on the creative quest. This has been a road upon which he meets and walks with me, though like those on the Emmaus road I often fail to recognize him until he breaks the bread of his presence with me.

Our discussion will begin with a brief overview of creativity in the Bible and some of the first faithful men and women who responded to that creative call. Next we will listen to the words of an ancient hymn (Philippians 2:6-11) and discover the incarnate shape of Christ-centered creativity. Finally I hope to apply some of these ideas to your life and mine, to our devotional lives and to our place in the community of faith.

Chapter Two

THE HUNGER FOR BEAUTY

"Frost on the window never the same / So many patterns fit in the frame

Captured in motion frozen in flame / And in the patterns is there a Name?

Why do we hunger for beauty?"

FROM A LYRIC BY JIM CROEGAERT

(1989 Meadowgreen Music/Heart of the Matter Music)

*L*ast night there was a visual feast in the sky. We waited out the dusk, my oldest son, Will, and I, straining to see who would discover the first star. Then, all at once, there it was! Just as our eyes were beginning to get used to the sight we looked over our shoulders and there was a dazzling full moon! It was as if, jealous for the attention, it had risen in all its glory to steal our gaze from that first bright star. We knew from an ephemeris that in a few hours there would be a full eclipse of this moon. Sure enough, a few hours later the earth's shadow began to creep across the pock-marked face of that jealous moon until it turned a deep brick red. To add to the drama, Mars was shining a brilliant red just below the moon. And for a finale, as if that weren't enough, we saw not one but two enormous meteors streak across the sky, each leaving a sparkling trail.

Whenever Will sees these kinds of astronomical wonders he whispers to himself spontaneously, "Oh, thank you, Lord!" When I called him out later to see the eclipse, he looked up through sleepy eyes and whispered, "Praise the Lord for the moon!" Will is not in the least what I would call a religious person, but he is someone who has always been preoccupied with power and beauty—I believe a God-given preoccupation.

The dome of the sky that warm summer night had become a cathedral for the two of us. Had we been in a cathedral made by human hands there would have been some huge icon on the ceiling. In our cathedral there was a cross in the cupola, not a hundred feet away but light years distant. It is known as Cygnus the swan or, in our case, the Northern Cross, and it flies straight down the Milky Way toward Sagittarius and the center of the galaxy.

As we follow the Milky Way down to what would be the western nave of our cathedral, there is the Archer, Sagittarius. He is shooting his arrow of stars into the distant and invisible heart of the galaxy. Tonight we have robbed mythology of him, and he is Jesus the Archer, taking aim at both out hearts!

A RESPONSE SHAPED BY BEAUTY

In the eastern nave lies the most distant object that can be seen with the naked eye, the Andromeda galaxy, the literal limit of our sight, the border to mystery. Tonight Will and I are seeing light that left that galaxy two and a half million years ago. Time and space come together as we look at the stars, as we worship silently together in this most massive cathedral of the summer sky. Something in both of us aches and hungers and is not filled even in the presence of this awesome beauty. This is more than a hunger for beauty. It is at the same time a hunger for love, for acceptance—which, if you think about it long enough, you'll realize is a hunger for God. For he is beautiful.

> *To gaze upon the beauty of the LORD . . . (Psalm 27:4)*

And that is why we hunger for beauty. Have you ever recognized your need for God in this particular way? Have you ever contemplated one of those long theological lists of God's attributes and concluded that he is above all beautiful? We rarely ponder his beauty, much less seek "to gaze upon it." Rarely does our theology include it in its outlines. But the beauty of God is a biblical reality. Throughout the Word of God he is recognized by and praised for being beautiful. All this my twelve-year-old innately understands by means of his childlike imagination. In fact, it would be impossible for him to imagine otherwise. The beauty of that night sky was a token, an icon of the beauty of God. By its beauty Will recognized it to be God's handiwork. God is beautiful. His beauty demands a response that is shaped by that beauty. And that is art.

> *The inspiration of art is a myth . . . which misreads*
> *the fact that art is worship into the fiction that art is*
> *humanity acting like God.* (CALVIN SEERVELD)

There is a voice that frustrates, befuddles and frankly terrorizes me every time I sit down to write anything, be it a letter or a song. Sometimes it sounds like my own voice; at other times I do not recognize it at all. These are the kinds of words it whispers:

> *"There is no conceivable way someone like you can create this."*
> *"How can you possibly hope to do better than ———?"*
> *"No one will listen or care what you have to say."*
> *"Aren't you too tired?"*
> *"What do you think you are, some kind of celebrity?"*

I argue with this voice. I try to ignore it, like the ringing in my ears. To date I have found only one way to make it go away and leave me alone, and that is to shift my focus. Look again at the things it says. Each statement has one thing in common: "you."

Creativity is not about me. It is not about you. It is not us somehow acting like little gods, creating on our own in the same way God creates. Although he asks us to imitate him, we are not imitators of God in this dimension. The most we can hope for is to respond appropriately and creatively to who God is and what he means. Creativity is a response.

In the early eighties many of us were embroiled in the post-Jesus-movement charismatic debate. The argument usually centered around tongues or the raising of hands. This was exactly what Satan wanted us to argue about, knowing that we would never arrive at the truth by asking those kinds of "technique" questions. And indeed most of us never did. We are still asking technique questions in many of our churches, or else we've given up asking questions at all.

The right question would have been, "How do we respond to God?"

RESPONDING IN WORSHIP

That is what true worship is—a response. That is what Bill Lane told me all those years ago. "True worship is a response to hearing God's Word," he said with an intensity I will never forget.

It's like romance—no, it is romance. When I first saw Susan, my wife, everything in me wanted to respond to her at every level: emotional, spiritual, relational, yes, especially physical. I saw. I responded. That is worship.

Creativity is worship insofar as it is, at its essence, a response. I hear the Word, and I respond with music, with silence, in adoration, in appreciation by picking up the basin and the towel. It is a romantic response to this Person whom I adore. He is beautiful! I want nothing more than to be in his presence. I love him! And so I sing and I write. If I could paint or dance I would do that as well. I forgive someone who couldn't care less about being forgiven. I try to reach out across the vast distance between me and my brother or sister.

Because it is a response, it does not originate with me. He speaks. He moves. He is beautiful. We respond. We create. We worship.

Perhaps we struggle to see the connection between worship and the call to be creative precisely because they are so intimately linked. We have forgotten that the call to creativity is a call to worship.

One of the most irritating accusations the voice I mentioned before can whisper is, "Do you think you're some kind of celebrity?"

By definition a celebrity is someone we celebrate. I looked it up. Just above the listing for *celebrity* I saw another word, *celebrant*. A celebrant is defined as someone who officiates at the Eucharist. A celebrant is focused on Jesus and his sacrifice. Interesting contrast.

Today I choose to be a celebrant. By God's enabling grace I will hold Jesus up before the world and not hold myself up. I will seek to respond to his extravagant love by any and all means possible. I will strive to create art that will communicate to the world, and most especially to him, how much I love and long for his presence.

BEAUTY AND LOVE IN CHINA

I had come to China on a cultural exchange visa, to perform at Beijing University on a Friday night. On the night before, I was notified that the concert had been canceled. There were no explanations. We were suspicious that the authorities had discovered the real reason we had come: to smuggle Bibles into the country.

Friday afternoon we received an invitation to come to the University anyway, to informally share with a few grad students. We were able to slip past one of the persons who are stationed at the front door of every building, watching and recording the comings and goings of everyone on campus. Once we were safely inside the basement we huddled together in a small circle. I shared a couple of songs but soon sensed that the students were more eager to share their experiences with me.

A young, intelligent woman shared her testimony in near-perfect English. She spoke of the spiritual struggle of growing up in the shadow of communism, where the official doctrine dictated against any belief in God. She told us, however, that ever since she was a little girl she had found her heart resonated with the beauty in nature. She described a series of epiphanies. First there was a sunset that caused a deep stirring in her soul that she could not put into words. Then there was a time when the simple beauty of the flowers in her mother's garden spoke to her of a simplicity for which her heart yearned. Simply by observing the beauty in nature she had become convicted of the existence of not simply a benign god but a loving, caring Father.

"Imagine the joy I experienced when I learned that he had a name and that it was Jesus," she said with tender, moist eyes and a brilliant smile. All at once almost everyone in the room began chiming in with nearly identical stories. In fact, I heard this same testimony again and again in China. What Calvin Seerveld refers to as the "hallelujahing of creation" is the whisper those Chinese students had all heard in their various encounters with the beauty of God's created order.

The order, the balance and the beauty of creation are indeed whispers, like the whisper that young woman heard in the garden. They are a shadow, like the shadow of the earth on the moon, which speaks of the essence of God. Such beauty draws us; it encourages and inspires us to worship. It even convicts us. The beauty of God demands a response from us. Maybe your response is a poem or a symphony. Better yet, your response might take the form of a new and creative way to show someone your love and God's. That was Jesus' favorite form of creative expression!

Perfect in beauty, God shines forth. (Psalm 50:2)

His relentless movement toward us, his romantic reaching out in Christ, embodies a beauty that is beyond words. Our God is beautiful in all his ways; it is a part of his perfection. This divine beauty has been woven into the fabric of creation, in the massive stars, inside the submicroscopic balance of the atom. Though we will only ever grasp his beauty in the most finite and rudimentary way, as creatures before a Creator, still it can be enough to incite an unconscious but uncontrollable desire to respond, to make our own personal world beautiful in its own way, to worship. Creative worship is one appropriate response to the heartbreaking beauty of God. The beauty of his presence can be recognized, reflected in the beauty of our songs and dances. It can be seen in the fabric of our daily lives. A thousand examples speak of a deep, inner hunger for beauty that, at its heart, is a hunger for God. We hunger for beauty because it is a beautiful God whom we serve.

A few weeks ago I received a call back from an old friend, the wonderful writer Brennan Manning. Conversations, even over the phone, with someone like Brennan are seldom ordinary. He had just finished reading through a five-volume work on Christian aesthetics by Hans Urs von Balthasar (hardly coffee table reading!). Brennan was moved by what he read, himself an intense hungerer for God and his beauty.

"In all those volumes, what was the most important insight you gained?" I asked.

Brennan was quiet for a moment and then, almost in a whisper, he said, "Love makes us beautiful."

That completes the circle, doesn't it? The God who is beautiful is love. His unqualified love reaching out to us through Christ is what makes us beautiful, and in response to that reaching out we hunger for more of his beauty. Out of that hunger we reach back to him through our worship, which calls us into new creativity. Beauty and love, two colors in the spectrum of the Light that is God.

—◊◊◊—

Chapter Three

THE CALL TO CREATE

*"Biblically speaking the making of art is not
an option but a command."*

HAROLD BEST

*E*ven though he had been able to put a name to each of thousands of animals the Lord had paraded before him, Adam could not find a name for the ache he was now feeling in his bones. Later, he would call it loneliness. But it must have been hard to understand the feeling of being lonely when what you are lonely for does not even exist yet. So before God created Eve, he must have created within Adam a lonely, empty place that was her exact shape and size.

When she is at last presented to Adam, her beauty demands a response and so Adam sings the very first song:

This is flesh of my flesh,

Bone of my bones.

In every way Adam could imagine, Eve was a real part of him. So now he has a partner, that one other single person who will make community and creativity possible. Eve completes and complements

Adam. She will make the creative process possible and pleasurable.

Adam's first lyric compliments and comforts her. It helps her to understand where she came from and where she is going as well as who she is. And all art, ever since, has sought to do nothing more. As the first couple, the first creative community, stand before their Creator King they receive the creative mandate:

> *Be fruitful and increase in number; fill the earth and*
> *subdue it. Rule over the fish of the sea and the birds of the*
> *air and over every living thing that crawls on the ground.*
>
> *(Genesis 1:28)*

This is more than a mandate to make a lot of babies, to become conservators of the earth. Neither is it a call to become "little gods," to somehow imitate God in the mystery of his limitless creativity. Rather, as romantic responders, Adam and Eve are encouraged not to answer back in some pale imitative way (real creativity is never imitative) but to give voice to their resonating hearts in praise. At its heart this is a call to worship.

HUMAN CREATIVITY BEGINS

The instruction to subdue and rule, as creature king and queen over God's creation, is a command to extend the image of God out into the world. They will create children who will carry on that image. They will plant gardens that, by their blooming, will perpetuate the rich creativeness and beauty of God. And they will, it is safe to assume, continue creating and singing songs to one another, like

Adam's first song to Eve. They will struggle to communicate their deep feelings to each other. And when Cain, Abel and finally Seth come along, Adam and Eve will, no doubt, sing them to sleep. They will write poems to help them understand who they are and where they came from. They will seek through their art to compliment and comfort them as well. And when the first gruesome murder occurs, it is not hard to imagine the first dirge of suffering and sorrow rising from the lips of those first parents. All these forms of creativity, even as far as the weeding of the garden after the Fall, performed in the presence of God himself in obedience to his mandate, represent the varied creative ways that people can give themselves, offer themselves up. And that is to say they are (or can be), according to our definition, forms of worship.

CREATE A BOAT?

The Old Testament's preoccupation with the creative process does not end with Adam and Eve. There follows a whole procession of men and women who are caught up, for better or worse, in this compulsion to create. We see them throughout the pages of Scripture in the throes of the creative mandate.

> But Noah found favor in the eyes of the LORD. . . .
> Noah was a righteous man, blameless among the people of
> his time, and he walked with God. . . . Noah did
> everything just as God commanded him.
>
> *(Genesis 6:8-22)*

In all of human history no one had ever experienced the aching hands and back Noah experienced. No one had ever been subjected to the ridicule he had heaped on him and his sons for the decades it took to build that ridiculous boat.

"Boat, what is a boat? For a what? A flood. Now tell me once again, what is that, and where does this stuff you call rain come from?"

Noah builds a remarkable and mysterious structure for an event that has never happened up till that time. There has never even been a gentle spring rain, the Bible tells us in Genesis 2:5-6, much less the deluge that is to come. Talk about imagination! Talk about inspiration! It is not difficult to visualize Noah stepping back from the monstrosity in his back yard, with the zebras braying and the monkeys chattering and the ducks quacking and the hyenas (as well as all his neighbors) laughing, and Noah saying to himself, "Where did this thing come from!"

From the old lady who fills a page with doodling as she talks on the phone, to the man who welds together dinosaurs in the middle of the desert out of wrecked car parts, all around us are examples of this mysterious, powerful urge (akin to the sexual drive) to create, to be creative, to live out or somehow respond to the beauty of our creative Father. Perhaps you can look at your own life and living room and see peculiar pots or pictures you've created because there seemed to be no other choice but to create them. People who cannot sing or play a note fill notebooks with songs. Others labor for decades over novels without the remotest hope of ever seeing them published. I am reminded of Richard Dreyfuss in the motion picture *Close Encounters,* tearing up his home, driving away his wife and children in the process of creating a huge scale model of Devil's Peak, according to an image the aliens had implanted in his poor unfortunate mind.

We are driven to create at this deep wordless level of the soul because we are all fashioned in the image of a God who is an Artist. When we first encounter God in the Bible, it is not as the awesome Lawgiver or the Judge of the universe but as the Artist. The language of Genesis is not flashy or grandiose; there is no waving of his great and powerful arm, no echoing of the mighty shout of the word of creation, no universe falling from his fingertips. Genesis tells us of his stepping back from the canvas of creation at the end of each day to examine his work and, like any painter or sculptor, with the utmost simplicity declaring, "Good." Like an artist he begins with the more fundamental forms. The light and darkness, the earth, air and water are his pencil sketch. Next he moves up in complexity until at the top of the whole wonderful heap stands humanity. "Very good!" is his verdict.

His image is woven into the fabric of everything we are. His thumbprint on our lives affects us in ways we will never even begin to understand. His divine beauty, which is part of our essence as well, demands a response. We see a majestic sunset, and a line of poetry comes to mind, or an image to paint, or perhaps we merely give a sigh that can sound like a song. Can a work like *Moby Dick* not be completely understood in such a way? Is it not an extended, amplified sigh from the pen of Melville in response to the beauty and terror he experienced while he was adventuring in the South Seas? Aren't the pages of such masterpieces merely signs that point us along in a direction toward the terrifying beauty of white whales or talking lions—and toward the God who created them? When we ask this question, or any question akin to it, we will inevitably discover that God has already answered it in his Word—answered it before we ever thought to ask.

The lesson for us to learn from Noah (which we will see even more powerfully demonstrated in the life of Jesus) for the sake of our own involvement in the creative process is that bound up with the creative mandate must be the notion of obedience. Genesis 6:22 tells us Noah did everything just as God had commanded. Beyond his abilities, his imagination, his common sense and probably his resources, we must see that it was the command of God that made the saving ark a reality. The command of God met the obedience of Noah, and the result was salvation. Sound familiar?

Indeed the command of God makes everything possible. As descendants of Noah, our very existence today demonstrates the truth of it. The command was met with costly obedience.

CREATIVITY ABUSED

After the flood was past, God renewed the creative mandate to Noah and his family (Genesis 9:1). Their creative response was to plant a vineyard that led to catastrophic consequences. Creativity abused! The abundance of the new vineyard led to the excess of Noah in his drunkenness. Perhaps he forgot who was the source of that abundant harvest. Maybe he wrongly assumed that after the ark he was "done" with obedience. Perhaps his excess of celebration pointed to his forgetting God. It is hard to tell.

In Genesis 11 we see another example, another response to the compulsion to create, only in this instance obedience has little to do with it.

> Then they said, "Come, let us build ourselves a city, with a tower that reaches to the heavens, so that we may make a name for ourselves and not be scattered over the face of the whole earth. . . ."

> So the LORD scattered them from there over all the earth, and they stopped building the city. That is why it was called Babel—because there the LORD confused the language of the whole world. From there the LORD scattered them over the face of the whole earth.
>
> (Genesis 11:1-9)

The deep, inner compulsion to create is clearly seen in the story of the Tower of Babel, as is the concept of the creative community. Only this is a creative community gone wrong, a group of people acting not in obedience but out of their own selfish ambition. This is community become industry. Unlike the story of Noah, here there is no mention of God's commanding the people. The tower seems to have been their own idea. The motivation was to make a name for themselves, and so their creative effort in mud, brick and tar sought to rob God of the praise. It had nothing to do with responding to or reflecting his beauty. It was solely a matter of power and fame for the industry of the people.

And the results were catastrophic. Humankind was divided and scattered. The curse, which in the end was a blessing, is felt by every one of us every time we seek to communicate with someone from another language group. And the confusion that was Babel has been reflected in every piece of art and music since. You and I listen to a new musical style and we respond, "I don't speak this language!"

Later in Exodus we see Moses' divinely induced preoccupation with the building of the tabernacle in obedience to God's command (Exodus 25—31). Here community is redeemed by and through the corporate creative process. Together the people of God create a space for God to dwell in their midst. It is the reverse of Babel. The community responds with generosity in providing the materials needed for the tabernacle. This was a selfless project, so unlike the industrial monstrosity of the tower.

One of the more remarkable features in the account of the tabernacle is the attention to detail: the precious metal for the post sockets, even the way the knots were to be tied. Scholars have observed that the tabernacle contained every type of representational art: painting, woodworking, sculpting, weaving, metallurgy, ceramics and more.

What is most amazing for the purpose of our study is a little-known individual named Bezalel.

Then the LORD said to Moses, "See, I have chosen
Bezalel son of Uri, the son of Hur, of the tribe of Judah,
and I have filled him with the Spirit of God, with skill,
ability and knowledge in all kinds of crafts—to make
artistic designs for work in gold, silver and bronze, to cut
and set stones, to work in wood, and to engage in all
kinds of craftsmanship. (Exodus 31:1-5)

Was there anything the son of Uri could not do? He is the first person in all of Scripture who was said to have been filled with the Spirit. And the underlying purpose is expressly tied to creativity! There is no mention of what he did before his experience with God. But now, in obedience, Bezalel becomes an artisan for God, equipped by the Spirit to create a place for God to "dwell among his people." Bezalel thereby played a part in fulfilling the deepest desire in the heart of God!

Bezalel's experience can be summed up in the two phrases God uses of him: "I have chosen" and "I have filled." His chosenness affirms the call of God on his life. His being filled indicates that he was given the gifts required to fulfill that call. The most special of his "giftings" was the ability to apprentice and train others, to encourage others to respond creatively.

The accounts of men and women struggling to be obedient to the creative mandate echo on through the early books of the Bible. Solomon builds the temple and later struggles to "find just the right words." Joseph uses his intuitive gift to interpret Pharaoh's dream.

Moses speaks on behalf of God and his people, and in response the people sing a song to honor him.

God is an artist and he is beautiful. He has woven his image into the fabric of our lives, which explains our drive to create things which are beyond us and which we don't always understand. Perhaps more important, he has issued a call to us that carries with it the possibility of obedience or disobedience: the call to respond to his beauty with creative worship. Our response cannot be centered in self, like the builders of Babel. We cannot afford to misuse our gifts. The Bible has shown us how costly that can be. God calls us to create a space in time for ourselves and others to meet with God, to gaze upon his beauty and to worship him.

Chapter Four

SINGING A NEW SONG

*I*t is the wee hours of the morning. Everyone is asleep but me. I have spent most of the day aimlessly moving words around on a piece of paper, taking inordinately long breaks to play games on my computer, telling myself I need to shift the focus for a while. Then, usually around two or three o'clock, when I run out of distractions, everything comes together. Often I realize in the middle of the process that I have not taken the time to ask for God's help or even simply stopped to spend time with him, to gaze into his face.

All at once the words start to make more sense than anything I could have ever come up with on my own. They fit the melody like a glove, as if the song was somehow preexistent and I am only just now hearing it. There is an experience of timelessness as well as I look at my watch and realize that what seemed only minutes in fact took four or five hours and the sun is beginning to rise. There in the early dawn I play through a new song for the first time, singing it to myself and to God, as the stars sang the very first song to him (Job 38:4).

As a songwriter I can tell you that the greatest moment of encouragement comes not from awards or high numbers on some soon-to-be-forgotten chart but from the singing of a new song for the very first time. To sing new words that have never been sung just so ever before, to play combinations of notes that have never been heard, to wonder as you're doing it whether they will have the desired effect on the listener, be it people or God—the sharing of the new song is an experience unlike any other.

The psalmist was preoccupied with the new song as well:

> *Sing to him a new song: play skillfully, and shout for joy.*
>
> *(Psalm 33:3)*

> *Sing to the Lord a new song; sing to the Lord , all the earth. (Psalm 96:1)*

> *Sing to the LORD a new song, for he has done marvelous things. (Psalm 98:1)*

> *Sing to the LORD a new song, his praise in the assembly of the saints. (Psalm 149:1)*

David understood this thrill as well. He knew that true worship was a response to God's beauty (Psalm 27:4), but most especially he realized the Source of all his songs:

He put a new song in my mouth, a hymn of praise to our God. (Psalm 40:3)

You can hear the childlike excitement in his voice in the words of Psalm 144:9: "I will sing a new song to you, O God; on the ten-stringed lyre I will make music to you."

In the entire section of the Old Testament known as the Wisdom Writings (Psalms, Proverbs, Job, Ecclesiastes, Song of Solomon) we see this excitement concerning the singing of a "new song." The simple act of writing and singing something brand new demonstrates that the truth contained in the Scriptures can now be placed in the heart of the community as they sing together the truth of who God is and what he means. By singing the new song they have made this truth their own. The new song, in a special sense, "incarnates" new meaning for the body of believers. By announcing at the opening of the psalm that it is in fact "new" the psalmist is reaffirming that, like the tender mercies of the Lord, so too the call to be creative has been given anew to the community by God. It is a fresh outpouring and, like the manna, should never be hoarded but rather collected and distributed in the right amounts to feed God's people.

REBIRTH OF THE SONG

In Scripture, whenever the kingdom is about to break through there is always a rebirth of the new song. In the first chapter of the Gospel of Luke, when the first gentle rumblings of the coming kingdom are being felt, Mary and Zechariah begin singing new songs. And when the momentous birth occurs it is first announced to the motley shepherds, again with a new song (Luke 2:14). Simeon, the first person to step from the world of the Old Testament into the New, from the world of faith as waiting to the world of faith as following, does so with a new song on his lips (Luke 2:29-35)!

Revelation records the complete breaking in of the kingdom:

> *And they sang a new song:*
> *"You are worthy to take the scroll and to open its seals."*
>
> *(Revelation 5:9)*

> *And they sang a new song before the throne and before the four living creatures and the elders.*
>
> *(Revelation 14:3)*

New songs are a major indicator that the Spirit of God is on the move, breathing, inspiring men and women to respond to his beauty for his sake as well as for the sake of the community of faith. New songs are a response to hunger, to God's desire to be praised for who he is and to the community's desire to be shown how to respond. By grace he gives us fresh material with which to worship him.

The psalmist understood this thirst. He sings of it again and again (e.g., Psalm 42:2). He understands that the thirst is as much a part of God's blessing as the song that temporarily quenches the thirst. Without the need, without the preoccupation for newness, there would be no motivating force for the song. The need of the artist and the needs of the community are crucial to the creative process. God's desire for worship (it is impossible that God should need anything) is part of the fabric of the call to create new songs.

When God's Spirit moves, he leaves singing in his wake, and in particular he leaves new songs, songs that embody his truth and are an obedient response to his beauty. These songs are a spontaneous and joyful response to the great truth that it is in fact God who is doing something new! He is coming, and his approach is meant to be strewn, like palm branches, with new songs!

Chapter Five

RECAPTURING THE IMAGINATION

RECAPTURE ME

Fleeing what I do not know
I flee to where I cannot go
Recapture me

The bridge between my heart and mind
You come across myself to find
Recapture me

You come and knock on imagination's door
You come to show to know you
Is what eyes and ears are for

With ears that hear but not receive
With eyes that see but can't perceive
Recapture me

Your paradox and poetry

They speak one sacred certainty

Recapture me

Through prophet's madness make me wise

Through foolish faith open my eyes

Recapture me

With sacred words, with silent words

You're the Living Word that must be heard

Recapture me

*I*nevitably our earliest memory is a creative/imaginative memory. Leonardo da Vinci's first memory was of being in his crib and having the tail of a kite come down and brush his face. He spent the rest of his life trying to learn to fly, both practically, by means of various flying machines and parachutes, and—perhaps more significantly— by means of his amazing art.

My first memory is of taking a walk with one of my cousins. It was early on a summer morning. The grass was loaded with dew. When she pointed out the dew to me, I got down on my hands and knees and focused on a single drop through which the morning sun was shining. It was brilliant with the light against the green grass. It seems from that time on I have been preoccupied with light—more exactly, with looking at and for light. It may be through the lens of a telescope, seeing the distant light of the stars, or reading in the pages of the Bible about Light that became a Person, someone who is at the same moment as distant as the stars and alive and shining inside me.

Before I could begin writing this book, or you could begin reading it, we first had to be able to imagine ourselves doing so. In reality, none of us can accomplish anything without first imagining it (except in the case of breathing I suppose), whether it's getting up from the sofa for a snack or building a rocket ship to Mars. For a split second we imagine ourselves reaching for a cup of cold water, and then we do it. We imagine which healing (or hurtful) words we might say to a friend (or an enemy), and then in the next instant, they are spoken, never to be called back. We imagine ourselves doing something, and then—in a tenth of a second or in ten years—we do it.

Our imaginations are involved in every area of our lives, in everything we do or say or are. It is no wonder that God is so intent upon recapturing them. Therefore, we must seek to understand the imagination biblically, that is, Christ-centeredly.

CAPTURING THE IMAGINATION

The imagination is the bridge between the heart and the mind, integrating both, allowing us to think/understand with our hearts and feel/emote with our minds. It is a vehicle for truth. Through the use of images, metaphors, stories and paradoxes that demand our attention, it calls for our interaction. The imagination is a powerful means for communicating truths about God, and so God shows an awesome regard for the imagination in his Word. I believe the human imagination is the door at which Jesus says he stands and knocks in Revelation 3:20—a door that we have the freedom to leave closed or open up to him.

Only a few verses later, as John's awesome vision begins in Revelation 4:1, his comment is especially meaningful: "After this I looked and there before me was a door standing open." Jesus knocked on the door of John's heart and mind. John opened the door of his imagination and received one of the most stunning revelations in Scripture.

Another way to grasp the power of the imagination is to realize that the sins that exercise the most control over us take place in the imagination. Jesus defined lust as taking place not primarily in dark alleys but in dark imaginations. Greed happens not when I make off with my neighbor's goods but when I imagine that they are mine. The author of sin in this world knows all too well the power of the imagination, so he too uses music, metaphor and vision for his grim purposes. He seeks to capture us as much as the Father seeks to recapture us.

Because we are called to creativity, a working, gut-level understanding of the imagination is vital. It can be our greatest strength or our greatest weakness. Sometimes it is both at the same time! To harness the imagination, or better yet, to bring it under submission to Christ is something about which we don't talk or pray or do enough. But before it can be redemptively used, it must be reclaimed.

"What is the experience of song writing like for you?" people often ask. In twenty years I have not been able to come up with an adequate answer. Sometimes I tell them it is like prayer. By this I mean that it primarily involves listening to God and to his Word. The only experience the writing of every song has in common is what I would call a sense of being burdened. Often there is a specific message with which I am burdened. More often, however, there is little or no specificity. What I am to say is not in the least clear to me. There is just the burden to say something. And God help me if I do not attempt to say it.

One of the Hebrew words for prophecy literally means "burden." The word *Masa* (מַשָּׂא), a burden, is used in Proverbs 30:1 and 31:1. Jeremiah 20:9 speaks of this burden as a "burning in the bones." Through the prophets we see God attempting to do what he will perfectly do through his Son and what he still longs to do in and through us: recapture our imaginations and set us on fire.

The narratives of the Pentateuch, though sometimes disturbing, are not all that difficult to understand. The poetry of the Wisdom writings, the songs and the sonnets still resonate in our ears much as they did in David's day. But the prophets—they are another matter entirely.

WHAT WERE THE PROPHETS SAYING?

The first obstacle to overcome is their "prophetic zeal." While we can relate to a cowardly Abraham, a deceitful Jacob or even a lovesick Solomon, what are we supposed to do with the passion of an Isaiah or the brokenheartedness of a Jeremiah? The zeal that consumed the prophets is foreign to most of us today, especially in North American Christianity. Who among us can truly relate to the prophets?

Perhaps most difficult is the way the prophets speak, the complex symbols of their visions, the bizarre images and metaphors of their songs. Are they speaking of times that have already come to pass, or are yet to come, or both at the same time? Is our call to decipher their prophecies as best we can? Are we supposed to try to keep record of their fulfillment as they happen? At the heart of it all, what is God really trying to say to us today through the prophetic literature? What are we to make of the prophets?

We must first realize that the prophets' burden was to call God's people to repent, to change their lives now. Their prophetic messages about the consequences that would follow if Israel refused to repent were not meant as mere signposts for the people as much as warnings of the dangers to be avoided. When the prophet spoke of fire from heaven coming to consume the unrepentant, the idea was not to sit looking toward the sky to see if the prediction would come true. No, the point was and still is, "Change your life now!" "Listen to the words of God as they pour from the prophets' seared lips!" "Open the door of your life to God!" The predictive element of prophecy is not the end but only one of the means.

Today our often unbalanced and unhealthy focus on the future predictions of the prophets (to the exclusion of their central call to repentance and a change of heart) has resulted in our missing their central point. We need to learn all over again that the goal of prophecy is "forthtelling," not "foretelling." But if the purpose is that simple, then why all the indirect communication, mysterious visions and metaphors? Why didn't God simply state his case before Israel and us and call for the faithful to come forth and take their stand with him? A simple demonstration of his power, followed by the choice of bowing the knee or burning, would seem much more to the point than all the bizarre activity and ravings of the prophets.

Doesn't the Pentateuch gives numerous examples of this kind of communication and how it ultimately failed to capture the hearts of men and women? Taking captive the human mind and heart involves more than fear or facts, emotion or knowledge. Through the prophets we come to understand that God is out to recapture all that we are or can hope to be—not just the mind or the heart but the mind of the heart, the heart of the mind, which is the imagination.

LISTEN TO THE WORD PICTURES

Being the Creator-Artist that he is, the great Romancer, the perfectly loving Father, God calls out to us, sings to us, paints images in our minds through the prophets' visions. These sounds and songs, these visions, stand at the door of our own imaginations and knock. Through them God opens the door of his own inner life to us. He paints pictures of his hopes for our future as well as his worst nightmares of what is waiting for us if we choose to go on living without him. He pleads for us to open the eyes of our hearts, to hear with our ears, to really understand. This is the heart of prophecy: God speaking to us in such a way as to recapture our imaginations.

The prophets teach us to learn from, to hunger for, to listen to God's voice. They acquaint us with the "how" of God's speaking. Through them we learn to listen to the whole of God's Word in new ways. By the prophets' example we discover that God is speaking through the parable of our daily lives, in the silence of prayer, in the good news of creation. They open our eyes to a vision as grand as the greatest of their own visions, to a world alive with God's speaking at every turn, in every moment, no matter how mundane it may seem. Through the prophets we begin to glimpse a God who loves us so much that he calls himself our Husband, who longs to embrace us as Father, who ultimately comes to us as Son.

I said earlier that one of the Hebrew words for "prophecy" literally means "burden." So how do the prophets respond to this burden they carry? They sing! Prophecy is almost always poetry. Many scholars believe that prophecies were often delivered to the accompaniment of live music (1 Samuel 10:1-16; Ezekiel 33:32).

The prophets use as their tools rich language and marvelous metaphors, the language of the imagination. Isaiah speaks of the sun and moon being ashamed; the trees clap their hands. God is seen as a Rock. In the prophets we also see God speaking through the bizarre activities of the prophets that called for an extra measure of obedience. Jeremiah hides his linen belt (Jeremiah 13). He breaks the clay jar (Jeremiah 19). Ezekiel constructs a toy town in the dust (Ezekiel 4). Hosea knowingly marries a prostitute (Hosea 1:2). The list goes on and on.

We can apply this understanding to our own creative efforts at many levels. On the most superficial level, we learn from the prophets that the tools best suited for communicating to the imagination are images, parables and sometimes even bizarre activity! At a deeper level, we learn that if we are to effect a permanent change in people's hearts, we must do more than simply teach them facts or reduce them to some emotional experience. Like the prophets, we must learn to reach out to the heart as well as the mind by speaking to the imagination. We must allow our audience the freedom to make realizations on their own, as with the parables of the prophets, particularly the prophet Jesus!

Chapter Six

A New Song to Christ

"Always the living reality of Jesus Christ revealed must be our rallying point."

CALVIN SEERVELD

*I*t's a steamy summer evening outside. Yet, even with the humidity, it is a beautiful night. The red glow of Antares, the heart of the Scorpion, reminds me of the summer heat. Owls and whippoorwills are hooting and singing their simple yet profound songs to their Creator. (Augustine said that there are two musical races in the world—birds and humans.)

Stretching out light years above me, the starry face of the sky seems to be silently smiling, embracing me as I walk in the comfortable darkness down to my little cabin to write.

THE SINGING STARS

Job speaks of the stars singing. Perhaps he had in mind the resonance that radio astronomers have only recently begun to listen to with the aid of their vast dishes. Or perhaps he meant the same kind of wordless song that only the silent light can sing. Or maybe it was just his way of saying that the magnificent beauty of the stars is a kind of song in itself.

The singing of the stars is a song I have sought to hear for most of my life. Sometimes, by faith, I believe I hear it, singing of and to the Creator. It reminds me of the vastness of who he is. If the stars are singing, as the Bible says they are, I am as certain as faith can be that they are singing a chorus to Christ, who made them and by whose immense, wordless power their mass is held together and kept burning so brilliantly. This chorus to Christ is a silent, wordless song, sung also with our lives and with whatever love we can lend to the chorus. It is an ancient, timeless, ever-new song.

In Revelation we read that a song will someday burst forth from all creation, from stars as well as starfish! Perhaps what I desire at the depths of my soul and strain to hear now is only the prelude, maybe even just the tuning up of the orchestra. When it does erupt, it will be a song that will never be forgotten—indeed, it will never cease to be sung.

Rarely do we know all we sing. I am continually learning from songs I have written. Sometimes we need to write and sing songs to help us remember important truths we tend to forget with time. Other times, songs enable us to put words to painful feelings, and just by singing them the hurt can be forgotten. So songs help us to forget as well as remember.

There was a time when the early church began to forget who Jesus was. It was badly in need of a song to help it remember. False teachers had crept in and were singing false songs about Jesus. There was confusion about the nature of his divinity. There were doubts as to the reality of his resurrection. People were losing sight of what his life had been all about.

THE ANCIENT MELODY

At the heart of it all, they had forgotten what the incarnation of Jesus really meant. In the midst of their struggle to remember Jesus, Paul provided them not with a theological tractate but with a simple, profound song that—in only one verse and a single chorus—told them all they would ever need to know about who Jesus is. This song is now ancient to us but ever new. As the fellowship, composed largely of older, retired Roman soldiers and their families, came together as quietly and unobtrusively as they could, we are told that there were Roman spies listening in. They overheard the Christians singing early in the morning and reported back:

> *They gather early in the morning and sing a hymn to*
> *Christ whom they revere as God.* (PLINY THE YOUNGER)

The ancient melody has long been lost, and so we need to listen to it anew in hopes of hearing a new set of notes. The early church called it simply the *Carmen Christi,* Latin for "hymn to Christ." This song is still important today for those of us who are struggling with our own crisis of remembering who Jesus is and what he means—for those of us who desire to sing a new song to Christ and to the world.

There is something about Jesus that we have forgotten but that the first hearers of this hymn still understood. A central part of the early church's confession of who Jesus is revolved around the idea that God created the universe through him. No fewer than three separate witnesses speak of this idea.

In John 1:3-5 we read, "Through him all things were made;

without him nothing was made that has been made. In him was life, and that life was the light of men. The light shines in the darkness, but the darkness has not understood it."

Paul repeats this important confession in Colossians 1:16-17: "For by him all things were created: things in heaven and on earth, visible and invisible, whether thrones or powers or rulers or authorities; all things were created by him and for him. He is before all things, and in him all things hold together."

And the author of Hebrews writes in 1:1-2: "In the past God spoke to our forefathers through the prophets at many times and in various ways, but in these last days he has spoken to us by his Son, whom he appointed heir of all things, and through whom he made the universe."

It is appropriate then that we look to Jesus in order to understand what creativity is all about, since the New Testament reveals him to be the author of creativity. Let's listen to the ancient hymn Paul sent to the church at Philippi. What did he intend the believers there to understand from it. What can we learn from it today? What will it help us to remember about Jesus? How can we sing it through our own creative lives?

Who, being in very nature God,

did not consider equality with God

something to be grasped,

but made himself nothing,

taking the very nature of a servant,

being made in human likeness.

And being found in appearance as a man,

he humbled himself

and became obedient to death—

even death on a cross!

—chorus—

Therefore God exalted him to the highest place

and gave him the name that is above every name,

that at the name of Jesus every knee should bow,

in heaven and on earth and under the earth,

and every tongue confess that Jesus Christ is Lord,

to the glory of God the Father. (Philippians 2:6-11)

The focus of the hymn is the incarnation of Christ. Do not be tempted to seek to understand the enfleshment of Jesus in technical terms; it's impossible. After all, the incarnation was an act of love, which means it's a mystery. At its heart, the song is telling us what it means to be created in the image of God. Verses 6-8 make up the single verse. It contains darker concepts: Jesus "made himself nothing." It speaks of his death on the cross. I have always "heard" the verse in a minor key. At 2:9 we move into an uplifting major chorus. It erupts with praise, speaking of exaltation, of every tongue confessing the lordship of Jesus Christ. This is where the congregation would have "sung out," at least as loudly as they could with Roman spies about.

The song has a formal structure that scholars refer to as a *chiasm*. It is based on the shape of the Greek letter *chi* or *x*. This is what the chiasm looks like:

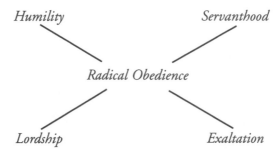

The top two concepts (humility and servanthood) are derived from verses 7-8 of the hymn. They represent the perfect starting place. At the nexus of the *x* lies the central notion of radical obedience, from the statement in verse 8 that Jesus was "obedient to death, even death on the cross." This completes the top portion of the chiasm and what would probably comprise the single verse of the hymn.

Finally comes the turnaround of the chorus, where the music must modulate from a minor to a major key. Here lordship and exaltation are shown to be the unexpected results of humility and servanthood, all because of the empowering force of radical obedience!

Paul wants his first hearers, and us as well, to see Jesus' life for what it truly represents: servanthood and humility. Jesus did not just talk about humility, it was the resonant tone of his heart. He did not merely command his disciples to become servants, it was the shape of his life as well. And as the nexus of the diagram represents, the concept of obedience is the key to the structure. Because of his radical obedience, Jesus, who was humble, will indeed be exalted. Precisely because he was the obedient servant, he is now Lord.

This radical reversal is seen every time the kingdom breaks through. The first are last and the last are first. Everything is upside down in God's kingdom. The poor are seen to be truly rich and the rich all but bankrupt. The wisdom of men is seen for what it truly is—foolishness—while the "foolishness" of the gospel disarms and confounds the "wisdom" of the world. In order to be mature we are called to become children once more.

This is all well and good. Indeed, it gives us cause to appreciate and praise Jesus for who he is. But, as he so often does, Paul has another purpose for his hymn. In fact he has wounded us from behind for our edification. Just when we thought it was safe to sing this impersonal and incarnational song we glance at the introductory verse (Philippians 2:5) and discover that this pattern of Jesus' life is meant to be applied to our lives as well. We are to have the same attitude, Paul says! What makes this truth unavoidable is that Jesus himself has already applied the pattern to our lives.

Does he not say in Luke 14 that "he who humbles himself will be exalted" (v. 11)? In our own lives within this upside-down kingdom, genuine humility (not the fake substitute we usually see) will someday result in our being rewarded by the Lord. And in

Matthew 20 Jesus tells the disciples, "Whoever wants to be great among you must be your servant." So for us, servanthood in this world will someday result in exaltation before God. Servanthood results in true greatness. The pattern of Jesus' life—humility, servanthood and radical obedience—must become our pattern as well.

HIDDEN IN CHRIST

"Your life is now hidden with Christ in God."

(Colossians 3:3)

"Which is the greater mystery, that man is artistically creative or that in his creativity he may empty himself and still remain artistic?"

(HAROLD BEST)

Where I live, when you look at the stars at night, you spend most of your time looking south. It is in the southern sky that you see the procession of the planets and the moon (and the sun for that matter) along an imaginary line astronomers call the ecliptic. All of the signs of the zodiac are there as well. So too are most of the interesting "deep sky" objects like nebulae and star clusters.

Alberio is a beautiful double star, one as blue as the sky and the other as golden as a wedding ring. Antares is the reddest star I know of, the heart of Scorpio. There is also an empty spot there in the southern sky, which I like to look toward and think about. Just in front of the constellation Sagittarius, at the tip of what is supposed to be his arrow, is the spot that marks the center of our own galaxy, the Milky Way. In every season the view toward the south is the most dazzling and inspiring view.

If you turn around and face north you will see a very different sky, a relatively dark one. No bright stars shine there, and few interesting nebulae or galaxies. Because of its position on the celestial sphere, this same set of constellations (the circumpolar constellations) rotates around an exceedingly dim, slightly green star. Polaris is its name. It is also called the North Star.

When sailors or even astronauts are lost, they look for this dim little star to regain their sense of direction. It is always in the same spot, the tip of the northern axis that goes through the celestial sphere. It takes a bit of time to learn to find it. People who don't know anything about the stars usually say, when it is pointed out to them for the first time, "Oh, is that the North Star? I thought it would be brighter."

NORTH STAR PEOPLE

People are sometimes described as stars. We look up to them, at their apparent brilliance, and feel ourselves small and insignificant by comparison. They move across the sky of life, luminaries, attracting most of the attention and admiration. Like the moon they constantly change their faces to suit the season. Like the sun they often burn hot. Like meteors they usually burn up quickly.

If you or I have any choice in the matter (and I am convinced that we do), I would like to campaign for the idea of our becoming North

Star people. Sure, we might not seem as bright or as interesting as some. Seldom will people point their telescopes at us. And when they do they will no doubt respond, "Oh, I thought she was brighter than that."

But as North Star people we can serve a deeper purpose. When people need us, we can be there for them, pointing the Way. While the world is spinning at a dizzying pace, we can remain grounded to the same spot, less dazzling but unmovable.

After all, Jesus was a North Star person. There was nothing in his appearance that seemed especially brilliant, according to Isaiah. In his time there were far more dazzling messianic stars who came and went with a flash. But Jesus has always remained there, rooted to the same place in the universe, unmovable. He constantly calls out to us to turn around and behold the dazzling dimness of his light, as it shines in this present world—to find our way to it, and then to find our way by it.

Chapter Seven

THE CHARACTER OF CREATIVITY

The three main themes found in the song of Christ represent the character of creativity. They are worth exploring further. These are not the traits we usually find in a powerful leader. Jesus set a very different pattern for us.

HUMILITY: THE GIFT OF HIDDENNESS

We have seen in chapter six that in the *Carmen Christi* the ancient Christians sang that Jesus "made himself nothing." What other character trait is as undeniable in the life of Jesus as his humility? Though he might have grasped equality with God, Jesus chose instead to become a humble servant.

Have you ever noticed how humble, unassuming and unmiraculous the miracles of Jesus are? The first one, turning water into wine, was recognized only by a few slaves at the wedding feast in Cana. "Go fill up those water jars," he said. Then, "Now take it to the master of ceremonies." Did you miss it? The miracle happened.

We could say the same about the feeding of the five thousand. There was no shouting, no waving of arms in the air, no hocus-pocus. Jesus simply prayed and passed the food out.

There was something indescribable about the way Jesus performed his miracles that always miraculously directed the attention away from himself and toward the Father. Jesus heals someone who is sick, and those who witness the healing inevitably "praise God." Jesus wins praise for the Father, not himself. "I can do nothing without the Father," Jesus said, thereby winning praise for God. Indeed, Jesus was not ashamed to confess his total dependence on God.

We have lost sight of true humility in our time. The best we know is a cheap imitation, "false humility."

"That was a good concert," someone will say to me.

"Oh no," I moan, "I sang flat, my guitar was out of tune . . ." This passes for humility. It is in fact only a disguised form of pride, a ploy to hear more compliments. At these moments I have forgotten who I am, and I look to strangers to tell me. I have lost sight of the truth of what Jesus has done in and for me. This is a perilous place to be, a dangerous trap.

Genuine, biblical humility is nothing more or less than knowing the truth of who we are in Christ. Only relationship with him can give us the genuine article. Jesus reveals to us two crucial truths about ourselves, and in the tension between these truths lies real humility. On the one hand he convicts us of our sin and fallenness, telling us our righteousness is really only filthy rags. And then in the next breath, smothering us with a big hug like the father of the prodigal son, he tells us how much we are valued, that in spite of our rebelliousness he loves us so much that he would rather die than live without us. That, then, is who I am. And that is who you are as well if you know him. We are men and women, boys and girls who are truly hopeless yet full of hope, truly lost but nonetheless truly found. We are shored up on either side so there is no room for false humility on one side or pride on the other.

Knowing the truth about who we are sets us free, for that, Jesus said, is the nature of truth. But being set free in an upside-down kingdom means being set free to become a servant. Before we were granted this freedom we were slaves to ourselves, that is, slaves to sin. Now, having been set free from ourselves, we are free to be slaves for Christ.

This newfound freedom is an experience of unveiling, of seeing not only oneself but also one's giftedness for the first time. "What do you have that you did not receive?" Paul asks. In the light of this new freedom of humility, of knowing the truth of who we are, we answer that our giftedness is not our own, it is from our creative Creator God. You and I stand unveiled as the simple recipients of a gift that is beyond ourselves.

KNOWING WHO WE ARE

This unveiling is, in truth, an opportunity to experience the hiddenness Paul speaks of in Colossians 3:3—to be hidden in Christ, to be free from pointing continually to oneself and instead point only to him. Here's a practical example of how it works.

I have a concert looming in the near future. I go to the hall full of myself, thinking only of what people will think of me. I have everything to lose since all that I am is riding on the success of the upcoming and as yet unrealized moment. As I begin to perform, the songs flow at first, but then as I play along, my mind starts to wander. "What are they thinking about me," I say to myself. Just then I learn the painful equation: thinking of yourself equals messing up.

Now let's look at the same example from another perspective. As I go into my concert I have a pretty good feel for my ability—that is, I know the truth of who I am in the whole scheme of things. I may not be the best musician in the world, but neither am I the worst. What does it matter anyway, since whatever gifts I have were given to me in the first place and are really not mine. So I can't lose. As I begin to play, my energy is not wasted on thinking of myself. The point of my playing is to present the message of the song, to "wash the feet" of the people or even God by faithfully playing my best with the ability I've been given. Now I become the beneficiary of another equation: to forget yourself equals the best possible performance.

Artists in medieval times did not sign their work. It never occurred to them to do so. (Michelangelo signed only one of his early sculptures, the *Pieta*—because he was incensed that some people were attributing it to another artist. He later deeply regretted his conceit.) Their art was a gift meant to point away from themselves and toward the God who gave it. They were safely hidden in Christ, free from the tyranny of the self. They knew the great truth that they were nothing more and nothing less than children of a great King who had been entrusted with a sacred task: to win praise for their Lord.

Knowing who we are is the hiddenness of humility. It is believing that the giftedness we may indeed possess is not of our own making, that the purpose of its being given is not that we might gain attention or praise for ourselves, but that we might respond in gratitude with our best creative effort to win praise for the One who first gave the gift.

OBEDIENCE: THE CALL

Long ago, in a garden, a great battle was lost when Adam responded to the call of God with the notion, "Not thy will, but mine be done." In another, darker garden called Gethsemane, we see Jesus struggling with his own will over against the will of the Father. Jesus is not fighting with a straw horse but with flesh and blood. In essence, Jesus comes into the battle saying, "If there is any way this cup can pass, if there is any way you can get me out of this, do it!" Knowing everything that lurks in the darkness before him, Jesus in his humanity says, "This is not what I want." What else does "nevertheless not my will but thine be done" mean if there was not a genuine conflict between two wills, Jesus' will and the Father's will, there in the garden?

The first seed of the victory won on the cross of Christ was sown in the garden. That seed was the radical obedience of the Son. The term "radical obedience" implies not doing what you want to do but doing the last thing in the world you want to do! "He was obedient to death," our song says, "even death on the cross." This can be called nothing less than radical obedience.

When we speak of obedience we must at the same time speak of the call, of vision, since we must be obedient to something or someone. In Jesus' case the call of God was to lay down his life for the many. And Jesus was radically obedient to that call.

This concept must be applied to the creative process. In a fundamental way the creative mandate is a sort of general call. We have seen that we can choose obedience or disobedience to this mandate. What remains in question is whether we are capable of a nonresponse to this deep part of our inner life.

In most cases an integral part of giftedness from God is not only the mechanical ability to paint or sing or dance but a deeper call. This call can be seen as part of an aesthetic value system, a system that helps determine what is beautiful and what is not. An artist paints by means of listening to this deep interior voice. A musician writes or performs in hopes of portraying the dimensions of this call. The vision provided by the call of God gives them eyes to see, ears to hear. It demands a response of obedience.

Haydn is said to have reflected, "Often when I was wrestling with obstacles of every kind, when my physical and mental strength alike were running low and it was hard for me to persevere in the path on which I had set my feet, a secret feeling within me whispered: 'There are so few happy and contented people here below, sorrow and anxiety pursue them everywhere; perhaps your work may, some day, become a spring from which the careworn may draw a few moments' rest and refreshment'" (quoted in Anthony Storr, *Music and the Mind,* p. 117).

GETTING PERSONAL

The call demands obedience on a personal level. It exists within the dimension of relationship, where true creativity always exists. In short, obedience to the call is obedience to God, and this represents a response of love. It remains to be seen whether one can be radically obedient to an aesthetic vision. It is doubtful whether something so deeply ingrained in our God-given image as the creative mandate can become the object of obedience on a level deep enough to be called "radical." It is more than an automatic or subconscious expression of our being created in God's image. But, within the context of relationship to the Father, the call demands a daily response of loving, personal obedience. It is a radical call, not to do something we want to do anyway, but to do the one thing we would least like to do in the entire world: die to ourselves.

Obedience is positioned at the nexus of the chiasm of the chorus of Christ. It mediates the power of radical reversal. It causes the servant's place to be transformed into greatness. It causes humility to be transformed to exaltation. It is what gave power to the life, witness and creative life of Jesus. And it promises to do the same in our lives as well.

SERVANTHOOD: THE BASIN AND TOWEL

And the call is to community
The impoverished power that sets the soul free
In humility, to take the vow
That day after day we will take up
The basin and the towel

> *"There is a difference between putting something aside
> and losing it. Christ showed us the difference."*
>
> (HAROLD BEST)

All along the way during that final journey to Jerusalem they argued about it: who was the greatest? Some described all the material wealth they had left behind. Others loudly mentioned their superior preaching ability. Others, ironically, boasted that their humility was the greatest among the Twelve.

Jesus had so longed to spend this time with them before he entered into his suffering. It was their last meal, their last chance to be together, and they were wasting it in the most colossal way.

Finally he had had enough. He did not lose his temper; he was too tired, too emotionally spent and too sad for that. Instead, without saying a word, he got up from the table. He had reached the point where he had given up on words. In his exhaustion he simply wanted to love them as best he could.

He took off his long outer coat, leaving only the seamless robe that the soldiers would be gambling for in a few hours. He took the towel Peter had been using to wipe off the table and wrapped it around his waist. Without a word he walked to the door and picked up the bowl of water that had been provided for washing their hands. By this time the Twelve were silent. They looked on, wondering what he was up to. Jesus' intensity told them not to interrupt by asking to help.

He began with Thaddeus, then Andrew, Philip, James, Matthew. By the time he got to Thomas there were tears in his eyes. They occasionally dripped onto the feet he was washing, like the tears of Mary on his feet a few days before. James, Matthew's brother, was next, then John; then, amazingly, Judas, who clutched his leather purse to his side during the process as if he was afraid Jesus was going to grab it away from him.

Finally Jesus came to Simon Peter, who by now was openly weeping from sorrow tinged with anger. His voice had been the loudest in the argument about who was the greatest. What Jesus did wounded him and angered him all at the same time.

"No," he muttered, "not my feet. Never!"

"Then we have nothing left in common," Jesus said, looking straight into his eyes. "You will not become a servant for me, and now you want to keep me from serving you."

Peter broke down at this point and wept like a little boy. It was embarrassing to everyone except Jesus, who had waited so long to finally see him break.

"Do any of you understand in the least what I have just done for you?" Jesus asked the silent, ashamed group. "When will you understand? You presume to say that I am your Lord. What now, then? I, your Lord, have washed your feet, have become your slave. Then what should you do?"

They never argued again about who was the greatest.

A POWERFUL PICTURE

The argument about who was the greatest seems to have been a common row among the Twelve. The story in the upper room is special because it represents the occasion when Jesus gave up. He had talked with them before about being a servant, but it seemed to have little or no impact on their lives. So now Jesus gave up on words and enacted a powerful parable for them.

"I came to serve and not to be served," Jesus says.

Paul sings, "He came in the form of a servant."

It is the shape of his life, the desire of his heart. If you do not know Jesus as the Servant Savior, you do not know him.

From looking at Jesus with the disciples in the Gospels, you would sometimes think he was their butler rather than their Master. When they are hungry, he feeds them. When they are tired, he is sensitive to their needs and takes them aside where they can rest.

John 21 contains one of the most touching examples of Jesus' care for the disciples. The incident takes place after the resurrection. John tells us that the disciples, at Peter's instigation, returned to their former job of fishing. Perhaps it was the only way they could feed themselves at this point. As they were making their way back to shore after a long night and no catch, they saw a figure standing on the beach. He called out to them the most irritating question you can ask any fisherman: "You haven't caught any fish, have you?" (Jesus specialized in irritating questions!)

The disciples responded, "No."

"Throw your nets to starboard and you will find a catch."

THE LORD OF ALL SERVES BREAKFAST

You know, of course, what happened next, but do you know the rest of the story? Do you know why he was there for the second catch of fish? We might expect Jesus to be standing on the shore in glory, with a host of angels inviting them to fall on the sand and worship him. That would be appropriate. But that is not why he was there. He was preparing their breakfast!

Though Jesus is the risen Lord of Glory, though he stands there with scars in his hands and feet and side, he is there to fix breakfast. He knows that they've been out all night, they haven't caught anything and they are hungry. And so he is there, their Servant Savior. He feeds them when they are hungry. He washes their dirty feet when they are tired. It is the shape of his life.

> *The more I think it over the more I feel that there is*
> *nothing more truly artistic than to love people.*
>
> (VINCENT VAN GOGH)

The disciples, like a lot of artists and musicians, argue, "Who is the greatest?" And Jesus rises, still hungry, from his own supper and demonstrates what true greatness is. In the upside-down kingdom, true greatness is found in the servant's kneeling with the basin and the towel.

"He came in the form of a servant," the chorus of Christ sings. What could have been more unlikely? This vision of Jesus as Servant Savior provides a foundation for a biblical value system. What is more valuable, to be served or to serve? "Whoever would be great among you must become a servant."

Though Peter protests, Jesus is insistent that unless Peter is willing to submit in humility to the servant lordship of Jesus, unless he is willing to obediently allow Jesus to wash his feet, he has nothing to do with what Jesus is doing. It is a stern word to Peter and to us.

Jesus longs to wash our feet, too, with the water of his Word, every day. He is serving us now, preparing a place for us in his Father's house, interceding for us before the Father. And in Luke 12:35 he promises to wait the table of the wedding supper of the Lamb—still the servant, still the same yesterday, today and forever.

The call to servanthood causes the creative gift to come alive. It gives it color and tone and direction and purpose. The art that naturally flows out of our obedient response to the call of God on our lives, as a result of the imprint of the creative mandate, can, by grace, become water to wash the feet of sisters and brothers, cold water to quench the thirst of an unbelieving world. To become servants of Christ is the highest goal we can aspire to in our creative work.

Whatever you do, don't be like Peter and say no to the One who longs to approach you and me and tenderly give us the washing we so badly need. That is simply pride, the kind of pride that gets you into arguments about who is the greatest. For we will never be able to pick up the basin and towel, or the paintbrush or the ballet slipper, until we have first submitted in humility to the Servant Lord.

WHO IS THE GREATEST? THE SERVANT

To be meaningful, art must serve, must wash feet. Like Jesus, who has been called "the man for others," our art, to have meaning, must exist for others.

The simple song that those frightened Christians sang, early in the morning two thousand years ago, has the ability today to put us in touch with who Jesus is and what he means. It provides the perfect categories for every artist and musician to construct a meaningful value system from which to create. It is a song we too must join in singing, even if there still are spies waiting outside the door.

Chapter Eight

A LIFESTYLE OF LISTENING

"Make a tree good and its fruit will be good, or make a tree bad and its fruit will be bad,

for a tree is recognized by its fruit.... For out of the overflow of the heart the mouth speaks.

The good man brings good things out of the good stored up in him,

and the evil man brings evil things out of the evil stored up in him."

MATTHEW 12:33-35

The Pharisees have hatched a plot as to how they might kill Jesus (Matthew 12:14). So Jesus withdraws to a less crowded, quiet place, where he can listen more intently to his Father. Listening to each other was the essence of Jesus' relationship with the Father. Often, the Gospels tell us, he would spend entire nights in prayer. Jesus also hopes this will be a place where the disciples will listen more intently to him.

During their retreat, Jesus heals a man possessed by an evil spirit, which prompts the astonished crowd to wonder out loud whether he might be the Messiah, the son of David. The Pharisees are not able to see or hear the truth about who Jesus is. Instead they try to connect Jesus' name with that of a demonic spirit, Beelzebub. This brings forth Jesus' stern mandate concerning the "unpardonable sin." Their blasphemy toward Jesus and even the Father will be forgiven, but to blaspheme the Holy Spirit is to burn behind them the only bridge to salvation. How can they be saved if they deny the only means for salvation? They thus render themselves "unpardonable."

OVERFLOW OF THE HEART

Where is all this venom coming from? What is its source?

In this incident Jesus seeks to illuminate where and how such unpardonable ideas are born. He speaks of their genesis in the heart. He tells of good men bringing good things out of a repository of goodness in the heart, and of evil men reaching down to find only evil to draw from their wicked hearts.

Jesus' conclusion regarding the source of these ideas is found in Matthew 12:34: "Out of the overflow of the heart the mouth speaks." The mouth is only a conduit for the heart and, like a tree, is capable of bringing forth only what its source allows.

For followers of Jesus, what fills the heart is determined by the quality of our devotional lives. The overflow of the heart is maintained by the time we spend together with God, listening in prayer, listening to the Word and straining to hear the parables of our own lives. It is the listening heart that is always overflowing with good things.

"The best way to show someone you love them is to listen to them," my friend Bill Lane told me once, on an unforgettable walk we took around the campus where he was a professor and I was a student. I was agonizing over my future wife, who, at that point, gave me little or no reason to hope that my affections would ever be returned. Out of my own impatience, I was preparing for a showdown with her, a confrontation that would have surely destroyed what little relationship we had.

"If you really want to show her you love her," Bill said with his characteristic intensity, "listen to her." I took his advice, and that girl has been my wife for twenty years.

Later I extended my understanding of this adage to my relationship with the Lord when I began to realize just how much I wanted to show him the extent of my love for him. If we desire to demonstrate our love for God, shouldn't we invest ourselves in listening to him? Isn't it true that he demonstrates his love to us by listening endlessly to our prayers?

There are three keys to developing a lifestyle of listening. The first involves listening to the Word of God. This is the most clear and authoritative voice we have. The second has to do with listening to the silence of prayer. And the third consists of listening to our own lives—first as poems, then as living parables.

LISTENING TO THE WORD

It is no accident that the heart of Judaism is contained in a creed called the *Shema*. This creed is the great central statement of monotheism. A devout Jewish person prays this prayer seven times a day. "Hear, O Israel, the Lord, your God, the Lord is One."

The first word is significant: "Hear!" Listen!

The Bible in general, and the ministry of Jesus in particular, has much to say on the subject of listening. Jesus said in Luke's Gospel, "Consider carefully how you listen" (Luke 8:18). And he was forever saying, "He who has ears, let him hear." For Jesus, it is as if our very lives depend on our ability and willingness to listen.

It may seem like an oversimplification, but basic to the art of listening is allowing the other person to speak, providing an open place in the conversation where they are granted the time, the space and the freedom to speak. As simple as this may sound, it can be a major task.

The same is true when it comes to allowing the Bible to speak for itself. We are to listen with as few presuppositions as possible, coming to the Word with the same sort of openness we might offer a friend who has let us know they have something important to tell us. In fact, that's just it—the Bible does have something important to tell us, if we will have the grace and wisdom to hear it.

When we find ourselves trying to listen to someone whose speech is slow or deliberate, the great temptation is to finish their sentences for them. The same is often the case when we listen to God's Word, particularly to those passages with which we think we are familiar. But one of the great proofs that Scripture is alive is its ability to speak afresh through passages I thought I knew by heart. In fact, I might have known them by "head," but not until they came alive in the heart had I really begun to listen.

Adopting a listening stance before the Word means keeping your mind as quiet as possible and letting the Bible finish its sentences, its stories. This will bring a new freshness into your time with the Word.

We fail to truly listen to the Bible when we read only for theological or doctrinal affirmation. The baptism of Jesus becomes a proof text for immersion and not a scene to which we are transported by our imagination. The crucifixion becomes a necessary piece of the puzzle for redemption, the obligatory final step in a long *heilsgeschichte* (salvation history), not a heartbreaking moment of transformation. Parables and visions become codes to break, sponges to squeeze dry and then move on. Richard Rohr says that parables do not lend themselves to extended analysis; they are a flash of insight or they are nothing at all.

Sadly, Scripture passages sometimes become simply fodder for lyrics or poems. There is nothing wrong with going to the Bible for the content of what we write, but when it is only that, like a thesaurus or a rhyming dictionary, we have a severe problem. I grieved for a song-writing friend whose Bible was only ever to be found on the piano!

In all these ways and more we effectively plug our ears to the voice of Scripture, which is in fact the voice of God. The simple act (which is sometimes not so simple) of quieting the mind and heart, and allowing the Bible to speak as if it had never spoken in its own voice to you before, will transform your time with the Word. Be quiet, be patient, and let it say what it has to say!

THE WORD

The Word is living
The Word is light
The Word delights my soul
Preserves my life
Holy and hidden
Forever new
The perfect sacrifice
Our Lord . . . Jesus Christ

The results of really taking seriously the command to listen can be surprising. Passages we thought we knew by heart speak to us in a whole new way. Stories come alive with the wealth of detail Scripture provides. All at once the text takes on a dimension of tone. We begin to hear a voice. We have begun to listen with the ears of our imagination, the most important goal.

In the ancient world all reading was done out loud. Everyone was taught to read in this way. Even when one was alone, reading was done audibly. That is how Philip knows what section of the Old Testament the Ethiopian eunuch was reading in Acts 8. These documents were written with this habit in mind, and we see examples of it all through Scripture.

Perhaps it might be helpful to start reading out loud to

He told them to stop trying to fight it. "Follow your mind wherever it goes," he said. "Follow it until it stops and then, wherever it stops, make that person or problem a matter for prayer. The struggling only leads to more noise and inner turmoil."

Most important is remembering that prayer is conversation and conversation involves listening, involves silence.

In stillness and simplicity
I lose myself in finding Thee
For you O Lord are close to me
In stillness and simplicity

LISTENING TO THE POEM OF YOUR LIFE

"We are God's masterpieces, poems . . ." (Ephesians 2:10)

Life is a song
We must sing with our days
A poem with meaning
More than words can say
A painting with colors
No rainbow can tell
A lyric that rhymes
Either heaven or hell

yourself. Hearing the sound of your own voice speaking the words of Scripture can have a stunning effect. Find new ways to hear the Bible, new ways to listen.

LISTENING TO THE SILENCE OF PRAYER

In stillness and simplicity
In the silence of the heart I see
The mystery of Eternity
Who lives inside of me

"To pray is to know how to stand still
and dwell upon a word." (ABRAHAM HESCHEL)

The ministry of Jesus was beginning to take shape. He had endured the temptation in the wilderness. He had survived the rejection of the people of his own hometown. His ministry of healing was well underway, having cast out demons, healed a leper and a paralytic. The time had come to choose the individual people he would pour the rest of his life into. There were already a number of "followers," but now the business of calling out an inner circle of disciples who could travel with him needed to be accomplished.

In Luke's Gospel Jesus never makes an important move without first going to prayer, and this time is no exception. We are told in Luke 6:12 that Jesus spent the entire night in prayer to his Father. When he returned from this extended time of listening to the Father, not only did Jesus know the names of the twelve he would "designate as apostles," he also had the outline for the new, completely unorthodox community they would begin building together. It is called the "Sermon on the Plain."

Over and over in the Gospels we see Jesus praying all night—in the wilderness, on the mountaintop, in Gethsemane. Though his divinity possessed the very mind of God, his humanity continually sought out the Father in all-night prayer sessions. In the account of those sessions we hear very few words, and so we can assume that there was much listening. But not listening for answers, for information. Prayer, for Jesus, seems to have been a time for simply sharing the presence of his Father, of listening to the silence of his breathing. When his cousin John is murdered, he flees to the arms of prayer. When he is confronted with the conflict of wills between his Father and himself, it is precisely to his Father he flees in the garden.

Jesus' life of prayer teaches us that we do not merely listen for words; we must learn to listen to the silence. For, as Mother Teresa said, "God speaks in the silence of the heart."

Can any of us say we know how to pray? Many books have been written on prayer, some of them helpful. For a time I was absorbed in reading books about prayer. But in the end I discovered that the best way to learn about prayer is to pray. And the best way to pray is to become a good listener and allow the Other to speak. We all have friends who dominate the conversation. Are you that sort of friend to God? After all, ask yourself, who has the more worthwhile things to say?

You're the Word who must be heard
By those who listen quietly
Is the reason we're not still
To hear You speak
Because we don't believe You will?

Sometimes it is helpful to break old habits. If your prayers long, simply pray the Lord's Prayer. The simplicity of it wi refreshing, and more time will be left for listening. Remember, J gave this prayer in response to the same petition that is on your he "Lord, teach us to pray." And so it is the paradigm for all prayers.

One of the first steps toward listening prayer is quieting your mi and heart. When your inner voice starts to chatter, repeating to yourse the verse "Be still and know that I am God" may help you to focus.

While I was at Western Kentucky University, Eberhard Bethge, the great biographer of Dietrich Bonhoeffer, shared with us a story of their days in the underground seminary. Bonhoeffer was discipling a group of young men in a secret underground seminary during World War II. (Hitler had closed all the seminaries.) The regimen required students to meditate on a passage of Scripture for two hours a day. After only a few days some of the men complained to Bonhoeffer that they were struggling with their minds wandering after only a short time. It was unreasonable, they told the amused Bonhoeffer, to require this of them when they had so many worries at home.

yourself. Hearing the sound of your own voice speaking the words of Scripture can have a stunning effect. Find new ways to hear the Bible, new ways to listen.

LISTENING TO THE SILENCE OF PRAYER

In stillness and simplicity
In the silence of the heart I see
The mystery of Eternity
Who lives inside of me

"To pray is to know how to stand still
and dwell upon a word." (ABRAHAM HESCHEL)

The ministry of Jesus was beginning to take shape. He had endured the temptation in the wilderness. He had survived the rejection of the people of his own hometown. His ministry of healing was well underway, having cast out demons, healed a leper and a paralytic. The time had come to choose the individual people he would pour the rest of his life into. There were already a number of "followers," but now the business of calling out an inner circle of disciples who could travel with him needed to be accomplished.

In Luke's Gospel Jesus never makes an important move without first going to prayer, and this time is no exception. We are told in Luke 6:12 that Jesus spent the entire night in prayer to his Father. When he returned from this extended time of listening to the Father, not only did Jesus know the names of the twelve he would "designate as apostles," he also had the outline for the new, completely unorthodox community they would begin building together. It is called the "Sermon on the Plain."

Over and over in the Gospels we see Jesus praying all night—in the wilderness, on the mountaintop, in Gethsemane. Though his divinity possessed the very mind of God, his humanity continually sought out the Father in all-night prayer sessions. In the account of those sessions we hear very few words, and so we can assume that there was much listening. But not listening for answers, for information. Prayer, for Jesus, seems to have been a time for simply sharing the presence of his Father, of listening to the silence of his breathing. When his cousin John is murdered, he flees to the arms of prayer. When he is confronted with the conflict of wills between his Father and himself, it is precisely to his Father he flees in the garden.

Jesus' life of prayer teaches us that we do not merely listen for words; we must learn to listen to the silence. For, as Mother Teresa said, "God speaks in the silence of the heart."

Can any of us say we know how to pray? Many books have been written on prayer, some of them helpful. For a time I was absorbed in reading books about prayer. But in the end I discovered that the best way to learn about prayer is to pray. And the best way to pray is to become a good listener and allow the Other to speak. We all have friends who dominate the conversation. Are you that sort of friend to God? After all, ask yourself, who has the more worthwhile things to say?

You're the Word who must be heard

By those who listen quietly

Is the reason we're not still

To hear You speak

Because we don't believe You will?

Sometimes it is helpful to break old habits. If your prayers seem long, simply pray the Lord's Prayer. The simplicity of it will be refreshing, and more time will be left for listening. Remember, Jesus gave this prayer in response to the same petition that is on your heart: "Lord, teach us to pray." And so it is the paradigm for all prayers.

One of the first steps toward listening prayer is quieting your mind and heart. When your inner voice starts to chatter, repeating to yourself the verse "Be still and know that I am God" may help you to focus.

While I was at Western Kentucky University, Eberhard Bethge, the great biographer of Dietrich Bonhoeffer, shared with us a story of their days in the underground seminary. Bonhoeffer was discipling a group of young men in a secret underground seminary during World War II. (Hitler had closed all the seminaries.) The regimen required students to meditate on a passage of Scripture for two hours a day. After only a few days some of the men complained to Bonhoeffer that they were struggling with their minds wandering after only a short time. It was unreasonable, they told the amused Bonhoeffer, to require this of them when they had so many worries at home.

He told them to stop trying to fight it. "Follow your mind wherever it goes," he said. "Follow it until it stops and then, wherever it stops, make that person or problem a matter for prayer. The struggling only leads to more noise and inner turmoil."

Most important is remembering that prayer is conversation and conversation involves listening, involves silence.

> *In stillness and simplicity*
> *I lose myself in finding Thee*
> *For you O Lord are close to me*
> *In stillness and simplicity*

LISTENING TO THE POEM OF YOUR LIFE

"We are God's masterpieces, poems . . ." (Ephesians 2:10)

> *Life is a song*
> *We must sing with our days*
> *A poem with meaning*
> *More than words can say*
> *A painting with colors*
> *No rainbow can tell*
> *A lyric that rhymes*
> *Either heaven or hell*

We are living letters
That doubt desecrates
We're the notes of the song
Of the chorus of faith
God shapes every second
Of our little lives
And minds every minute
As the universe waits by

The pain and the longing
The joy and the moments of light
Are the rhythm and rhyme
The free verse of the
Poem of life

So look in the mirror
And pray for the grace
To tear off the masks
Find the art of your face
Open your earlids
And hear the sweet song
Of each moment that passes
And pray to prolong

Your time in the ball

Of the dance of your days

Your canvas of colors

Of moments ablaze

With all that is holy

With the joy and the strife

Of the rhythm and rhyme

Of the poem of your life

Of the rhythm and rhyme

Of the poem of your life

God speaks through the Word of Scripture, through the silence of prayer, but also through your life. Your life is a poem—and a song, and a parable.

LISTENING TO THE PARABLE OF YOUR LIFE

The Bible gives abundant examples of people's lives that were in fact living parables. Abraham offering his son to God, a parable of God offering his own Son for us. Jacob wrestling with God, a parable of the struggle we all have in finding faith. Job's suffering, a parable about the truth that God doesn't always give us answers, but he always gives us himself.

Listening to the parables of Jesus will teach us how to listen to the parables of our own lives. The best way to learn to listen to the parable of your life is to examine the parables of Jesus and learn how to first listen to them.

The parable is not simply one form of communication; it is a paradigm for communication. A parable is an extended metaphor that has, through extension, come to life with characters and a story. A metaphor simply says *a* is like *b*. A parable is able to enlarge the statement: this is how *a* is like *b*, and this is what that means or can mean for you. The extension of the metaphor into parable allows for us to be included in the story.

We identify with one or another character in a parable. You may feel like the son who had strayed off with the family riches. I may see myself in the older son who is jealous of the big welcome given to the prodigal. Perhaps you are the woman who has been searching on her hands and knees all day—perhaps even all your life—for the treasure of a single lost coin. The parable draws us in, forcing us to participate or get out altogether. A simple metaphor could never do all this.

Most of the parables of Jesus exhibit a lack of closure. Yes, they have endings. The boy returns home, the judge finally listens to the widow, the pearl is found. But the moral of the story, the summation, the conclusion is often left unstated. Within the freedom of the form of the parable, Jesus leaves the "aha" to us. The moment of realization is ours to savor, and if we explain the parables to death we rob them of this, their most important characteristic. The transcendent "aha" moment of the opening of the eye of the heart is to be experienced by you alone with the Spirit.

Like parables, our lives often lack closure. We need to heed the invitation to listen! For it is still Jesus who is creating the story as you live day by day. As with the parable, you are invited not only to be a character in the story but, more important, to identify with the other characters in the parable that is your life. Through identification with others you will experience to the full all that the parable of your life means. Again, answers are seldom given, but the One who is the Answer is always ready to give us himself. The moment of realization, of illumination is left to us, in sovereign freedom, to savor alone with the Spirit.

It occurred to me the other day why parables work at all. It is because truth has been woven into the fabric of creation. Everyone understands the word pictures of a seed falling into the ground, of a parent loving a child, of a person anxiously searching for something valuable that has been lost. From such basic creation facts, eternal lessons can be drawn by means of parables.

It is our devotion to God that is the true source of creativity, maintaining the "overflow of the heart" out of which we speak. But never lose sight of the fact that is it God who has first spoken and who speaks. If he is speaking, then nothing else matters except listening.

Listen to his Word!

Listen to the silence of prayer!

Listen to the poem and parable of your own life!

But the "aha" doesn't always come easily. The frustrated disciples asked, "Why do you speak to the people in parables?" (Matthew 13:10). In the tone of their question I hear, "Why don't you just say it straight out, Jesus?" It is a frustration most all of us share with the disciples not only as we seek to understand the Bible, but also as we strain to hear God's voice in the parable of our daily lives. There is so little "straight-out" language in the Bible or in life. But it is so for a purpose.

There is a lot of straight-out talk in the Law. But the apostle Paul points out that hearing it did not seem to have much effect on fallen ears, beyond telling us, like a rigid schoolteacher, how hopeless we truly are. The rest of Scripture—the Prophets, the Psalms, the narratives of the Gospels, the visions of Revelation—speaks to the imagination, to that bridge inside us between the heart and mind, that doorway to the soul. Imagination is what enables us to think with the heart and feel with the mind, a task Jesus seems intent on our learning to do.

That's why when God speaks it is so often in a vision, a parable, a metaphor or a song. These are ready vehicles for the imagination. What we have called the devotional life is nothing more or less than the process of listening to God through all the various means he has chosen to use in speaking to us: the Word, prayer, life. The source for our creativity is the overflow of the heart, the result of our devotional life. In the call to be creative, a call that goes out to all God's children, we sense the call to listen to him and, in childlike naiveté, to imitate our Father by creating works that will magnify his praise.

As Brennan Manning has said, "If God is speaking, then nothing else matters but listening!"

Chapter Nine

THE CALL IS
TO COMMUNITY

"And I myself will be a wall of fire around it," declares the LORD,

"and I will be its glory within."

ZECHARIAH 2:5

A community (*cum,* with; *moenia,* fortifications) by definition is
a place with protective walls. It seems we are always talking about
"breaking down walls," walls between races, between sexes and so on.
And certainly these barriers do need to come down. What we don't
talk enough about is the building of walls—walls to protect our
brothers and sisters, walls to redemptively keep out certain aspects
of the world. We need protective walls, which is to say we need
community, which is to say (according to Zechariah) that we need God.

JESUS AND COMMUNITY

If Jesus is our pattern for the creative life, we need to realize that one
of the most deliberate things he did was create community. In fact he
created at least three communities. First there were the Twelve,

deliberately chosen. This group would be the vanguard. They were the ones who were given the authority to spread the "good news." It was in the give-and-take of this small community that the Twelve found themselves transformed, certainly most directly by their interaction with Jesus, but also from the "iron sharpening iron" that sparked and scraped between them. After all, among the Twelve there were educated and uneducated, rich and of modest means, nationalist and traitor. And yet, with all their disparity, within the context of community these frail men were transformed into fearless champions of the new faith. They found within the context of community a challenge to their creative abilities as they shared the gospel, engaged their differing cultures, lived out among themselves the mystery of who Jesus was, found new ways to reach out to and understand the mystery of one another.

A second, more intimate level of community existed between Jesus and the three "pillars," James, Peter and John. These were the disciples to whom Jesus revealed the deeper aspects of his true character. We need to realize, however, that these three didn't receive more attention from Jesus because they were somehow more intelligent or faithful. The truth is they got more attention from Jesus because they needed more! Whenever they opened their mouths they consistently said and did the wrong thing. Peter rebuked, corrected and eventually betrayed Jesus. James and John, the first and last to die, lost their thunderous tempers and selfishly vied for thrones on either side of him.

Yet in their frailties there is a deep lesson: our giftedness or lack thereof is not what determines our closeness to or usefulness for the Lord. That is based wholly on his gracious choice. It doesn't take a rocket scientist to look at either the Bible or the contemporary church and realize that the Lord seems most intent on using what is most frail and faulted. This fact is seldom remembered in the rarefied air of the creative world. The strength of our community comes from our corporate weakness, which is made strong and creative only by the grace of Jesus.

A third level of community was the little-mentioned "seventy," a group it seems only Luke was much interested in (Luke 10:1-4). This larger group of "disciples" was responsible for paving the way before Jesus arrived into a given area. This explains why, when he arrived, there was so often a large crowd ready to hear what he had to say. Within the context of his ministry it would seem that such a large number of men and presumably women as well would be unable to spend much time with Jesus. It would be interesting to know how many of them had even spoken intimately with him at all.

The point is, Jesus was given to the creating, sustaining and utilizing of community. It was a sustaining force to his person and ministry. And it provided the foundation for the church universal that he said he would build.

COMMUNITY THROUGH THE CENTURIES

Community goes far beyond the church, of course. Historically, the greatest periods of creativity have been the result of community. The Renaissance, that great flowering of creativity, faith and imagination, was largely the result of the coming together of communities or schools of artists. Da Vinci, Michelangelo and practically every other artist of name was a product of a creative community or "school." In the context of such a school, which usually centered around a single "master," the young artist would be apprenticed for a period of months or years. Da Vinci, for example, was part of Verrocchio's school. His earliest recognized works are "contributions" he made to paintings that were the products of two or more artists within the school.

One of the most striking examples is "The Baptism of Jesus" by Verrocchio himself. In the painting a thoughtful John the Baptist is pouring a bowl of water over Jesus' head with one hand while precariously balancing a long staff in the other hand, which also grasps an unfurling scroll with a Latin inscription concerning the Lamb. John is busy with his baptismal duties; Jesus is gazing down in thoughtful reverence. In the lower left area of the picture two angels are kneeling. One looks like a small boy with a golden halo, but the other actually looks like an angel! It is luminous. Somehow it appears even holier than Jesus! This is the figure the twenty-three-year-old da Vinci contributed to his mentor's work. One wonders whether, if there had not been the encouragement of this collaborative community, the world would have ever known the singular genius of Leonardo da Vinci. (When Verrocchio saw the figure he vowed to never touch paints again!)

In such early schools creative input was given within the context of community, that is, within a context of respect and trust. The community encouraged a high degree of excellence and an aesthetic accountability. The freedom to experiment and even to fail was a vital part of the experience of every young apprentice. The image of the lonely, tormented artist came largely with the modern era. Even though we speak of "schools" of Impressionism, the character of these random collections is radically different than the products of the Renaissance schools. They might best be described as a gathering of individuals and loners. The existence of what we would refer to as genuine community was almost totally lacking. Several artists, most notably Vincent van Gogh, missed the kind of collegiality such communities would have afforded.

CREATIVE COMMUNITY IN THE BIBLE

The Bible gives several examples of creative communities. In the Old Testament the music and craftsmanship of both tabernacle and temple worship came out of the community of artist-priests. Within the community of tabernacle craftsmen, Bezalel was the "master." As the phenomenon of prophecy grew, schools or families of prophets came together, presumably with the prophet of name as the master. Remember that Old Testament prophecy was almost certainly accompanied by music, so these prophetic schools were involved with prophetic music as well as words.

In the New Testament, as music passed from the professional priest-musician to the amateur lay-musician, ecclesia became the center for new hymnology, for corporate worship. Art and music were created in response to the needs of the community for new vehicles to contain its worship. The body of Christ became the repository for a vast wealth of creativity. Community called creativity forth. To encourage community is to encourage creativity. Art, music, mercy and every form of ministry seen in the body are responses to the needs of the community. The need for kindness, beauty and truth all cry out for the creative fingerprint in each of us to respond, to wash the feet of the brothers and sisters with our various creative gifts.

There are practical as well as spiritual reasons why creativity flourishes in community. Today's "industrial" approach to music and art by and large goes against this common-sense approach. The best way to view this stark difference is to compare the gifts of community to creativity against industry's denigration of the same gifts.

> Gauguin says that when sailors have to move a heavy
> load or raise an anchor, they all sing together to keep them
> up and give them vim. That is just what artists lack.
>
> (VINCENT VAN GOGH)

CONSTRUCTIVE CRITICISM

Though most artists find it difficult to admit, criticism is vital to an ongoing, developing creativity. Art should not, in fact cannot, happen in a void. It requires give and take between the members of a community.

I experienced this dynamic when I began writing songs. I was a member of a small biracial church in Bowling Green, Kentucky. The pastor began giving me the outlines of his sermons, asking if I would try to come up with songs or choruses. Whenever a song did come, I was able to first share it with him, receiving input, primarily in regard to the lyrical content. I was also given immediate input from the membership when the song was performed for the church at large.

What is most important here is the context in which the interaction happens. For me the advice came from men and women whom I loved and deeply respected. Their words, even when they were critical in a negative sense, came in a context of support and trust. If they criticized a song, it was to help me write a better one next time. And so the songs—not only my own but those of the other writers in the church (and there were several)—gradually improved over time. The criticism was truly constructive—that is, by it we were able to "build" better and better songs.

In the commercial, industrial world, criticism usually takes place after the fact, in a public forum (e.g., reviews in magazines). This type of criticism is rarely constructive. Its source is often someone unknown to the artist and therefore difficult to trust. It comes too late in the creative process to be of any use. Criticism that comes from industry is meant to merely tell the consumer which product to buy. The artist and the community are all but forgotten.

APPRENTICESHIP

An apprentice is one who is involved in an ongoing relationship for the purpose of improving his or her artistic craft. Because it is such a basic and helpful notion, apprenticeship exists in several other fields outside the artistic community, such as plumbing and auto mechanics. Unfortunately, in the past several years, for reasons we will look at in a moment, the notion of apprenticeship has been waning in the creative community.

Apprenticeship reminds us once again that creativity does not occur in a vacuum; it requires a community. From apprenticeship the community acquires new artists, artists who have been spared innumerable dead ends because a "master" has taken them in hand and passed on a wealth of experience. And thereby art grows and develops.

Apprenticeship is discouraged in the industrial world for two reasons. First, the commercial system is based on individualism (celebrityism). Second, production schedules rarely afford the time required for someone to be nurtured in his or her craft. In the absence of community, the artist experiences a sense of aloneness and defeat.

AESTHETIC ACCOUNTABILITY

We talk a lot about accountability these days. Primarily we bemoan the moral failures that happen because of a lack of accountability. But all around us are "creative failures" as well, due to the fact that artists are often trying to create outside of the aesthetic accountability that only community affords. Once again, the ability to render and receive accountability is based on relationship, respect and trust. These are values of community.

In the context of industry, aesthetic accountability becomes the responsibility of the individual artist and tends to be shaped not by any absolutes but by what seems to be successful in terms of commercial success. Immediate success usually wins out over what would be aesthetically more beneficial. Once more the artist is alone in a creative vacuum.

FREEDOM TO EXPERIMENT

Also vital to the ongoing growth of any creative person is the freedom to experiment, that is, the freedom to fail. Artists must be free to try seemingly foolish things, experiments that at the outset seem doomed to failure, if for no other reason than to be able to discover on their own what does not work for them. When the dust from the debacle clears, when the cacophonies stop echoing, artists need to know that their acceptance, their value as a person, has not been damaged in any way. So what, try again. The community will always be here for them.

Within the drab confines of commercialism there is little room to experiment. A limited number of "visionaries" are allowed. Their freedom to experiment most often comes from past successes. Due to the risk involved in carrying these individuals, the industry can afford only a few of them.

UNQUALIFIED ACCEPTANCE

Akin to the above notion but still deserving separate mention is the notion of acceptance. In order to maintain their equilibrium, artists must be able to trust that, regardless of their ability to perform, they are still fully accepted. They are not more loved because of their hit record, nor are they any less loved because of their recent flop.

Acceptance of this kind is based on a completely different value system. It holds that more is not necessarily better—that love and acceptance are gifts, by grace, not by works.

Acceptance is won in the commercial realm based on a value

system founded on quantity over quality, expediency over craftsmanship, salability over vision. Relationship, trust and accountability are concepts not commonly seen. As we consider the crisis in creativity within the church today, a restoration of biblical community is crucial. The believing community is the safe nest in which the biblical value system is protected, nurtured and hatched. The artists among them, fledglings from that nest, are taught to fly within the safety of a flock, but to fly all the same.

> *The making of an industrialized society will extinguish the meaning of the arts, as humanity has known them in the past, by changing the conditions of life that have given art meaning.* (DONALD DAVIDSON)

A MODEL FOR CREATIVE COMMUNITY

Looking at a model for a creative community may be helpful. Let's call it the "Covenant Artist Alliance." Marie-Alain Couturier once wrote in *L'Art Sacre:*

> *As for us, we shall state again our most profound conviction: outside of the faith nothing allows us today to foresee a genuine rebirth of Christian art. We say "outside the faith" to emphasize that a really living Christianity forever keeps within itself (for art as for everything else) the unpredictable resources of life. But this we can affirm in the faith alone and in the faith entirely pure; outside of*

it there is nothing that justifies any hope. Everything is too
distorted, too garbled. In a world whose economic,
intellectual, and social structures—and for the most part
the religious structures as well—are in direct opposition to
the poetic and the mystical, how could a living sacred art
be reborn except by a miracle?

This proposed alliance does not represent an indictment of the current state of the contemporary religious music. Rather, it provides an alternative, a safe haven for both current artists and those who are to come. There presently exists no mechanism to help disciple the next generation of musicians. This model might provide such a space.

The purposes of the Covenant Artist Alliance will be these:

1. To provide a structure for genuine community.

2. To provide a covenant to which artists and their supporting resource people can commit themselves, uniting them in purpose and vision.

3. To provide a means of aesthetic accountability within the community.

4. To provide a place where apprenticeship can happen.

5. To support a speaker series and forum for the community at large.

6. To provide a retreat center for covenant members.

7. To place in community artists and resource people so the spirit of the covenant can be lived out in the day-to-day "business" of creativity.

The vision for the structure of the alliance is twofold. The core will be the covenant artist groups (limited in size to perhaps four or five members). These groups will commit themselves to discipleship in its three basic forms: discipling someone younger; walking with someone side by side; and being in a mentoring relationship with someone older (the Timothy, Paul and Barnabas model). This commitment will be spelled out in the covenant.

Alongside this group will be associate members. These are the primary resource people for artists. It is good to include this group in the alliance for two reasons. First, this group is often excluded from artistic communities, leaving them to feel like "second-class citizens" when in fact their practical gifts make it possible for the artists to do their work. They have much to offer in experience. Their inclusion is why the organization can be called an alliance. Second, the presence of associate resource members will provide a co-op atmosphere. The image of everyone bringing their different gifts together, writing, playing, producing, marketing and distributing, is a thoroughly biblical one. The purpose is found not in the profit motive but in the strengthening and deepening of the community.

Finally, here is the covenant on which our alliance can rest.

THE COVENANT

We believe in
God the Father, Jesus the Son, the Holy Spirit

The servant lordship of Jesus Christ, his birth, life, death
and resurrection as told in the whole of Scripture

The body of Christ, his church

The existence of God's call and purpose in the individual
life of the believer

The necessity for that call to be lived out in community

The truth that the Christ-centered life is
shaped by servanthood, humility and radical
obedience (Philippians 2:6-11)

Chapter Ten

LETTERS TO CHRISTIAN ARTISTS

*I*n 1966 the Dutch theologian H. R. Rookmaker published a book on art that had, in its final chapter, a letter to a Christian artist. With the kind permission of *Christianity Today*, I have reprinted that letter. Later, it occurred to me that I should ask a few friends whose advice I would covet to write letters of their own. Every person who responded did so joyfully, excited to take part in encouraging young artists. If I could ask anyone on earth for advice and encouragement, these wise and loving men would be the ones I would ask. It is with great delight that I share their wisdom with you. I encourage you to read them slowly, one letter at a time, allowing a space of time between each one for the different ideas to simmer on the back burner of your mind.

Harold Best

I first met Harold Best when he was still the head of the music department at Wheaton College. I read his then-new book *Music Through the Eyes of Faith* and was deeply moved by his confessional transparency. The man I soon came to know as a friend validated every word of his insightful book by the way he lived out his life before the students who still love and revere him. When asked to write this letter he agreed if I would also allow him to write a letter to senior pastors. "That is a letter that needs to be written!" he said with a smile.

Dear Friend:

I, too, am an artist, although it is hard for me to think of myself primarily this way. I mean, I have been trained as an artist and have some sort of surging passion within me about the arts, particularly music, and I have an incurable hunger for the things of high quality, even to the point where I succumb to the sin of assuming that those who do not company themselves with the best art must not, after all, be deeply spiritual. While I have intellectually and theologically come to the point of refuting the equation of truth and beauty, I still find myself entangled in the temptation to reunite them, if only to prove my own spiritual depth and to confirm the shallowness of those who choose what I have labeled mediocre.

Try to avoid this temptation, for it can eat away at any conception of the true, in-Christ unity of his church. As denigrating as bad taste is and as much damage as it can do to the human spirit, God rises above this, refusing any aesthetic intermediary through which to view and value us. The only intermediary is Jesus, who takes us purified into the company of God, irrespective of our art. Meanwhile, let's do all we can to raise standards and to rescue people from groveling in mediocrity, but let's not create any false equations between a people's standing with Jesus and what kind of art they like. Don't forget that while Jews were being gassed and incinerated, their tormentors were listening to Mozart and Beethoven, and returning home to dote on their wives and children.

I don't know how real you feel about yourself. I don't know how many people have "gotten to you" with their assortment of messages as to who artists "really are," how they should behave and to what particular camp they should properly belong. I do not know whether you have made art into Art and artists into Artists, or whether you have come to a wise understanding that no human endeavor, no matter how noble and magnificent, should ever be capitalized. So these questions: Are you truly pleased with yourself as to the simple and lonely fact that God decided to create you in a certain way? Do you understand that he has been both mysteriously near and far as you have been making your way through the wonder of human imagination, the darkness of sin and the clean, clear washing in the blood of Christ? And have you so surrendered your art to your Savior that were he physically to walk in on you and speak directly to you, you would not change anything you are now doing?

Here are a few more things that I think about and ask you to do also. I hope that I am not wrong. If so, write back and help me out.

Your authenticity does not depend on proving to people or to God—

with pitches, paints, or pen—that you really are quite a piece of work. Rather, I pray that you are discovering that your authenticity lies in who you are constantly becoming in Christ, and that you make art because you cannot keep yourself from the simple joy of shaping something as best you can and then pouring it over Jesus' feet. The only reason for doing our very best, despite any cost, is the infinite worth of Jesus, for making art this way is where authenticity lies.

Remember that only God can imagine and make something out of nothing. In this sense, he is the only One who deserves the title of Creator. We are merely creative. That is, we can only imagine and make something out of something else—something that has already been imagined and made, whether in the creation itself, or from the work of creative people. This means that you are not to consider your work as much original as individual. You work will always be "out of" what you have somehow come across and "into" what others will eventually come across. Thus, don't be afraid to borrow, but be sure you borrow the best and grow from the borrowing. Then you will understand this simple fact: The best artists begin by being influenced and end up influencing. Finding yourself is not a creative soliloquy, a narcissistic look into a private talent pool or some kind of aesthetic privatism. It is, instead, finding others who themselves have found others who in turn have found still others, joining humbly and hungrily with this vast community, then seeing the difference that individuality has made all around you and praying that you will end up making enough difference to warrant your citizenship in the same community.

Even so, don't shun greatness or be jealous of it. Look to it and learn from it, but do not covet it, for this will take your creative eyes off of what you are inherently capable of and will turn you into a strident and self-engaged stylist. Remember the great Sebastian Bach, who spent twenty-seven years at St. Thomas Church in Liepzig, not striving for greatness, but simply getting ready for Sunday. At the head of many of his compositions he wrote the Latin initials for "Jesus Help" and at the end, "To God Alone Be Glory." Let this hard working servant be called great as civilization eventually measures greatness, but don't forget the larger fact that, at base, he was simply a good man going about his daily work with all his might. Chances are, you will not be great. But you can be good, and you can dwell lovingly with goodness. In this way, you will be found at the clarifying center of a civilization's soul. And if through your prayers, your work, and your example, you can persuade others that they too must keep company with goodness, then just maybe our rankled and riddled culture will find healing and mending.

Don't just be the artiste, be a good craftsman. Remember that God makes things beautiful from the inside out while we usually make things look good on the outside no matter how tawdry they may be on the inside. The down-deep interior of a redwood or a geode or the DNA molecule or, for that matter, our own body, is a song of elegance. But look behind the usual piece of art—whatever the medium—back into the seams, joints, and interior framing, and you will often find an embarrassing pastiche, a lack of craft, a disdain for interior wholesomeness, all covered up and slicked over by exterior gloss—what uncaring people see or agents and publishers contact for. Try to make your work elegant from the inside, out, as if this were the only way to examine it, and in so doing you will join up with the mind of the One in whom are hidden all the treasures of wisdom and knowledge.

No matter how good you are, no matter how much your admirers make of your work and seek your company, remember this: You are not all there is, even within the stylistic territory you may dominate. There are other territories, ones you may not be able to hold a candle to, and you must turn toward their particular worth, be further schooled and more deeply advised by them. You must, in turn, give your devotees a much-needed lesson in artistic width by telling them—no, imploring them—that as much as they love your art, they are severely impoverished if they do not seek to love that which to them may at first be unattractive or "not their style" or "not meeting their needs."

Furthermore, even though you have decided to explore as many kinds of art as possible, this is still not enough. Be interested in as many things outside of the arts as possible. Fill your day and your mind and your surroundings with curiosity. Find out how a steam engine works; find out why some buildings fall and others stand; find out why airplanes fly and why Kierkegaard was able to write the way he did; find out how a plow works and how the same law allows an airplane to fly and a boat to sail into the wind; find out why chaos theory is so theologically elegant; find out what Chomsky meant when he said that children are born bringing the sentence with them; we just give them the words. Love a horse and talk to plumbers. Ask questions of everybody, and don't hide your ignorance, for ignorance is simply the unlit side of curiosity and the outside of the door to wisdom and knowledge. Be a limitless person to others and maybe you will stretch them more than your art does. Let's hope.

There is a profound difference between making and begetting. Don't make the paganizing mistake of saying that you are your art, that it has somehow come out of your loins, that it is, amazingly enough, an extension of you. Artists, even the best of them, do not beget their art; they do not give birth to it, as if incarnationally they were in their art or as if their art were in their image. This is misguided and hyperinflated romanticism. It has no more place in your mind than it does in God's mind. Be simple and straightforward about your art. Don't mysticize it; don't mysticize your relation to it. Love it, yes, just as God loves a zebra. But don't outstep him by saying that you are your art when he can't say that he is a zebra. We must guard as much against panthropism (man is his art) as we do against pantheism (God is His creation).

Furthermore, remember that the greatest work of art ever, say, a Mona Lisa or a Taj Mahal, is of infinitely less worth in God's eyes than the persons who made them. Elevating a work or art over the worth of its maker is just as wrong as elevating the artist over other people. Art and artists are just one strand in the vast creational weave. Learn the decency and worth of the work of a farmer or a longshoreman or a physicist and then let your art stand cheerfully and humbly alongside their work, but not above it. Here's a test for the elitists: If saving the life of an AIDS-ridden waif in a barrio or rescuing an embryo from abortion is not more important than saving the Mona Lisa from destruction, then your elitism stands.

Pursue excellence, but don't yak about it all the time as if your words were your justification for your art. It just doesn't work that way. How many times have you heard third-rate artists defend what they're doing by taking up the shield of excellence? This not only switches your attention from the art to the words, but it consigns the words to the same trash heap as the art deserves. "I am pursuing excellence" is a neat thing to say, but it doesn't guarantee a thing. It is simply some kind of witness to an attitude. If the attitude is one of seeking out, tasting and joining with the very best there is, then the slogan has merit. However, doing this just might mean giving up on making art, or at least making it public. Never mind. God has plenty else for you to do. In the meantime, you can still enjoy the primary privilege of making your art only for the Lord. Sing in the bathtub and forget the public. You don't need a public in order to sing to the Lord, and God will not be downgraded because the art you privately offer him isn't up to snuff. Remember, he sees (hears) it perfected in Christ in a way that escapes our imagination.

Don't hide behind ministry as a way of highlighting or even sacramentalizing what you are doing. To an authentic Christian, ministry is simply another word for living a life of constant worship and witness. So don't separate ministry out as if it brings special luster or mystique to the ordinary acts of service, whether through your art or your daily chores. Don't forget that the little boy Samuel had it right when the Scriptures describe him as ministering to the Lord. This is another way of talking about Mary (or one of us) pouring perfume over Jesus' feet. True ministry is, above all, to the Lord. Going about it this way relieves us of placing so much dependence on what we do and authorizes us to depend on what only Jesus can do. In other words, our ministry is truly ministry when we move the responsibility for its effectiveness from the gift to the Giver, from the action to the Actor. There is a world of difference between your art being expected to minister and the Lord being expected to minister while you make your art. Once this is understood, art then can become fully itself instead of being shaped according to what we think will minister. The former is freedom and the latter is often no more than maudlin market research sprinkled with holy water.

Don't forget the children. If you are a singer, attracting large audiences and selling mucho CDs, and if in the meantime you are abusing your voice, remember this: countless admiring children—teenagers among them—will adopt your abuse as their norm. If you are doing this, don't speak out against drugs, tobacco or child beating until you have cleansed your own throat.

If your talent or marketability is such that you could easily go on the road all the time, think twice. Think about fame as a 100 percent efficient way of disappearing as a simple individual and joining the mythologized world of exaggeration and oversize. Think instead about the value of staying home and becoming what our culture so sorely needs: a local, hometown hero. This means spending your time as a demythologized servant, one whom little children can play basketball with, youth groups can learn from and senior power-pastors and music committees can be corrected by.

Remember that the most natively diverse people in our culture are very little children. These smallish images of God can at once learn several languages; they can as easily fall asleep or dance to Bach as they can to Cajun, Prokofiev or Satchmo. They "know" somehow why the ancient Egyptians or Picasso drew people and trees the way they did; they improvise constantly; and they keep asking "Why?" Don't join those who, *along with their warped educational systems, narrow all of this down into set routines; who pretend, along with all of the Disneyfiers, that reality is just a cartoon away or just a few magic steps down some kitschy castle path. Let the little children thrive in the wonder of being made in the image of God; lead them to Jesus by whose powerful word and from whose endless imagination a thousand shapes, textures, colors and sounds erupted in those first days of creation. In one of the most exciting of all of education's paradoxes, try to keep up with them even as you lead them, and don't be surprised if their faith and their frankness outstep yours. Above all, take the same care of them that Christ-in-you would take if he and you were to change places.*

With high hopes for you,

HAROLD M. BEST

Makoto Fujimura

I first "met" Makoto Fujimura by way of an insightful article he had written for a collection on the topic of Christianity and art. Later I discovered he was an artist in New York City, the founder of a movement there called the International Arts Movement. We corresponded several times, Mako always providing generous words of encouragement or endorsement and finally the foreword for this book. His gallery was only a block or so from the World Trade Center. After the terrorist attacks of September 11, 2001, I confess, I was afraid to e-mail him, fearing that there would be no response. This silence went on for a couple of months. Finally, we reestablished contact on a live radio show for the Moody Broadcast Network. What a relief it was to hear the sound of his gentle voice coming over the phone lines.

Dear Young Artist:

Remember your first love—how much you enjoyed creating as a child. If you ever lose that sense of joy, you will need to reflect on why you lost that spark. Of course, the craft of expression takes much "dying to self" and much discipline. A discipline of any form takes perseverance. But when we are going through a period of training, we must remember the reason for our training. Our journey needs to have a specific direction.

C. S. Lewis writes, "God became man to turn creatures into sons: not simply to produce better men of the old kind but to produce a new kind of man. It is not like teaching a horse to jump better and better but like turning a horse into a winged creature" (Mere Christianity, *p. 167*). *The gospel of Jesus is not a message that we can be trained to run faster and jump higher in a race of moralism. The cross of Jesus stands because we cannot possibly meet God's standard of righteousness and goodness. We cannot even keep our own promises, let alone God's commands. "But God demonstrates his own love for us in this: While we were still sinners, Christ died for us" (Romans 5:8). Jesus' love for us can only be received as a gift. Only when we rest upon him does he give us wings, to hover between heaven and earth. These wings are gifts of grace, but they must be aligned to God's direction and purposes. Our journey will begin in a*

Garden and end in a City. We are headed toward the City of God.

In Jesus, becoming like a child is the first step in learning to fly with God. Jesus himself became a child first and became our elder brother, so we can be part of his full inheritance, his freedom. To be joyful in creating requires that we understand what it means to be a child of God and to take advantage of our inheritance. Lewis continues in the same passage, "But there may be a period, while the wings are just beginning to grow, when it cannot do so. . . . The lumps on the shoulders . . . may even give it an awkward appearance."

To the world the "lumps" of our inheritance as a child of God may look strange and unnatural. Your teachers and your friends may not fully understand your intuition to respond to God. But you still must. This is all part of learning to fly. Your "lumps" are the seedlings of vast treasures we will receive in the kingdom to come. But many, including those in the church, will not understand. When Mary poured her expensive perfumed oil upon Jesus' feet, Judas and the other disciples responded, "What a waste!" In the same way the world may see what you do and see it as too "outside the boundary of . . . " or too expensive. Be daring, even dangerously so, as Jesus was daring and dangerous to conventionality.

An artist's true work is to enjoy God. Artists help us all in our flights of grace. Strict moralism has never produced great art. Like Mary's expensive oil, our expression flows out in response to God's work in our lives. Even artists who are not aware of God can benefit from our response. Perhaps they will be the ones to create great art, but we need not worry about that. We need to focus on our intuitive response to God, as it is pleasing to God. Jesus commended Mary: "Leave her alone. . . . Why *are you bothering her? She has done a beautiful thing to me. . . . I tell you the truth, wherever the gospel is preached throughout the world, what she has done will also be told, in memory of her" (Mark 14:6, 9).*

Jesus' commendation connects the task of bringing the gospel in to the world (the Great Commission) with her beautiful, devotional act. Our intuitive acts in response to God are for others to witness. Remember that Mary's oil was the only thing Jesus wore to the cross. A friend of mine said that in the aroma of Christ, Mary's oil mixed with Christ's blood and sweat, there are da Vincis and Bachs floating about. Art helps to prepare the way for the word of God to be proclaimed. Artists are vital for the church, because their creativity and passion expose a language to communicate the gospel to a dying world. But you must first understand your call to be a servant in your local church before you can expect the church to understand and embrace your creativity.

We must lead the way for our brothers and sisters, exhibit the joy of repentance, articulate the love for our Lord and envision a church that is alive with the Holy Spirit. Spend much time reflecting on the Word. Sit at the feet of the Savior and listen to his voice. Don't be a critic when you create. You can look at your work later and discern what is good. Let your mind and heart be filled with God's Spirit. Your growth as an artist is not in being able to impress others and God. Rather, growth comes by understanding how limited you are. Learning to use your wings means learning to accept the narrow path and allowing God to speak through your specific limitations. This process of shedding the unnecessary will take time, and it will seem very unnatural at first, even awkward.

Pray. As Simone Weil wrote, "Absolutely unmixed attention is prayer." Artists know instinctively the artistry behind the prayer of the faithful. Pray that our imagination be "baptized." Pray through your materials "thy kingdom come." Go into galleries and museums and pray. Pray for artists, pray for museum curators, pray for collectors. Pay attention to what God is telling you even through artists who deny God. After all, they "know" God enough to deny him. We may learn more from the world's artists about the true condition of the world than from Christians. By listening to their stories, we can also help them find the fulfillment of their journey in the gospel. Because our story (of the gospel) is the Ultimate Story behind all stories, our prayers can be the catalyst revealing the hidden truth behind their art.

A child of God knows that "creation waits in eager expectation for the sons of God to be revealed" (Romans 8:19). The whole realm of nature waits for our arrival onto the stage of life. God "frustrates" creation so that the very groaning of life produces expression by children of God. In the theater of life, we see in the darkness and suffering all around us a world that beckons for our arrival. Our creative endeavors are mandated to begin with that understanding of suffering and darkness. Art helps us to confront darkness head-on. For that reason, we must continue to create in order to announce our arrival on the stage of life. We need to help our brothers and sisters articulate their suffering. We need to be willing to sacrifice and through that sacrifice give birth to a true community.

Further, by "showing up" on the stage, what we announce may be a key to unlocking someone else's story. A child of God knows that he or she is loved. And because of that love, which exceeds our own love, we can move out to take risks in creativity. Love is the ultimate fruit of the Spirit, and it will not grow apart from total dependence on the Lord. Art, ultimately, is expression of that love. Therefore we cannot create but by sacrificial love. We need to redefine art and its effectiveness by how it helps us to love one another sacrificially. Fear and terror, no matter what form, will destroy our creativity. Even when we cannot paint or write, love is available to us as the ultimate expression of God's art.

"Good art," Dr. Bill Edgar points out, "obeys the Ten Commandments." Remember that the Ten Commandments begin with God's love for us. God has already delivered us out of Egypt. We need to understand, then, God's commandments as they apply to our lives and our art. This is a lifelong journey of discovery and sharing in the community of God.

We are either for him or against him. The commandments are sharp, double-edged swords that force us to examine our lives and our motives in all endeavors. "He who is not with me is against me, and he who does not gather with me scatters" (Matthew 12:30). We cannot stay neutral to the reality of God. Trying to stay neutral will always end in the Lord's rebuke: "So, because you are lukewarm—neither hot nor cold—I am about to spit you out of my mouth" (Revelation 3:16). Go into the art world being bold and assertive in the power of the Holy Spirit. God will do the rest, redeeming culture and humanity.

MAKOTO FUJIMURA

Hans Rookmaker was professor of art history at the Free University of Amsterdam, Holland. He died on March 13, 1977, at the age of fifty-five.

During the Second World War he was imprisoned at Scheveningen by the Nazis and kept in solitary confinement for three months. According to Dutch law, he was provided with a Bible, and it was at this time that he began his journey with Christ. In 1943 he was deported by the Nazis and sent to a concentration camp and finally to Stanislau Prison in the Polish Ukraine. After the Russians liberated Stanislau, Rookmaker returned to his home in Holland.

His house eventually became a gathering place for young students. At the same time, he began speaking at youth conferences. He was noted for his willingness to talk with young questioners till the wee hours of the night. Despite his fame as a scholar and author, he was known as a humble and down-to-earth servant of Christ. The letter that follows is his response to a letter he received from a Christian artist.

Your letter reached me yesterday after its trans-Atlantic voyage, and I propose to answer you directly. Your request touches on a problem I have been thinking about for a long time. Maybe what follows can be of help to you. I'd like to approach the matter in a schematic way, pointing out some principles.

Your questions concern your wish to paint—that is, to work as an artist—as a Christian. It really is remarkable that you decided to do this when you were just converted. Many times new Christians just drop their aesthetic careers because they think painting and art today are incompatible with being a real Christian. I'm glad you made this decision and hope to help you by suggesting the following principles for Christian artists:

1. If God has given us talents we may use them creatively—or rather, we must use them creatively. A Christian artist is not different from, say, a Christian teacher, minister, scholar, merchant, housewife, or anybody else who has been called by the Lord to specific work in line with his or her talents. There are no specific rules for artists, nor do they have specific exemptions to the norms of good conduct God laid down for man. An artist is simply a person whose God-given talents ask him to follow the specific vocation of art. There may be circumstances when love towards God would forbid certain artistic activities or make them impossible, but the present moment in history does not ask for such a sacrifice. Quite the contrary. We— the Christian world and the world at large—desperately need the artists.

2. To be God's child means to be offered freedom—the Christian freedom Christ himself and Paul in his letters say much about. This freedom is most important for anybody who wants to do artistic work. Without freedom there is no creativity, without freedom no originality, without freedom no art, without freedom even no Christianity. This freedom can exist only if it is based on love towards God and our neighbors, and if we become new men through the finished work of Christ and the Holy Spirit is given to us. Without this base, freedom may easily mean being free from God and consequently free to indulge all the cravings of the sinful heart of unredeemed man. (For more on this matter of freedom, see Paul's letter to the Galatians.)

Christian freedom is different from humanistic freedom, the freedom man gives himself to build a world after his own devising (as we tried by the Enlightenment and the humanists development after that time in the Western world). Humanistic freedom leads to all kinds of problems, as our Western world is now learning from experience. Freedom in the biblical sense is in no way negative—shun this, don't do that, you must leave that alone, keep away from this. Christian freedom has nothing to do with a set of rules by which you must bind yourself; indeed, such rules may easily be pseudo-Christian. Freedom is the necessary basis for creativity, for creativity is impossible when there is timidity, when you allow yourself to be bound by narrow rules. Do not think the modern art world is free—but we will turn to that later.

Freedom is positive. It means being free from tradition, from the feeling that everything you do has to be original, from certain fixed rules said to be necessary in art—but also from the thought that to be creative you must break all kinds of rules and standards.

Freedom means also that there are no prescriptions for subject matter. There is no need for a Christian to illustrate biblical stories or biblical truth, though he may of course choose to do that. An artist has the right to choose a subject that he thinks worthwhile. But nonrepresentational art provides no more freedom than the most involved allegorical or storytelling art.

Freedom includes the right to choose your own style, to be free from tradition but also from modernity, from fashion, from today and tomorrow as well as from yesterday. Yet there is no need to slap the contemporary in the face, as some streams of art nowadays deem necessary. Christian freedom also is freedom from the sinful lust for money, from seeking man's praise, from the search for celebrity. It is freedom to help a neighbor out and give him something to delight in.

3. There are norms for art that are a part of God's creation. Without them art would be an empty name without sense. To say a person has been given a feeling for art and beauty (everybody has, to a certain extent), that he has been granted a strong subjective sense of artistic rightness, is but another way to say that he has been given an understanding of certain norms God laid down in his creation, the world in which we live. We call this taste, a feeling for design and color, the ability to grasp the inner harmony of a complex of forms and colors, the understanding of the inner relationship among elements of the subject matter, the ability to recognize the indefinable dividing lines between poor and good art, between worn-out symbols and fresh ways of saying things that are important to man.

These norms do not stand in the way when we want to live in Christian freedom; they are a part of our world and our nature. Only when man revolts and does not want to be a creature, when he wants to be God and not man, does he feel bound to these norms. For those who love the Lord and rejoice in His good and beautiful creation, these norms provide the opportunity to live in freedom and to create. As one cannot act and live free as a woman if one is not a woman and has not the possibilities of a woman, so the norms for beauty and art are at the same time the opportunities to see beauty and create art.

4. When God created—and in that way made the perception of beauty and the human creation of art possible—he gave art (or any artistic endeavor) a place in this world in which we live; and that world

he called good. (I added artistic endeavor because we have to think not only of the rarefied museum type of art called Art with a capital A today, but also of all other types, including ceramics, dance, music, pictures used in Sunday schools, and so on. We shall come back to this.) Art is here because God meant it to be here.

So art has its own task and meaning. There is no need to try to justify one's artistic activity by making works with a moralistic message, even if one is free to emphasize moral values. Nor is there any need to think one has to serve as a critic of culture, or always provide eye-openers to the non-artists, or teach, or evangelize, or do whatever other lofty things one can think of. Art has done its task when it provides the neighbor with things of beauty, a joy forever. Art has direct ties with life, living joy, the depth of our being human, just by being art, and therefore it needs no external justification. That is so because God, who created the possibility of art and who laid beauty in his creation, is the God of the living and wants man to live. God is the God of life, the Life-giver. The Bible is full of this.

Art is not autonomous. "Art for art's sake" was an invention of the last century to loosen the ties between art and morality; that is, to give art the freedom to depict all kinds of sins as if they were not sinful, but simply human. The human understanding of depravity, of morality, of good and bad was thereby undermined or erased. The results we are seeing today, in our century. The meaning of art is its being art; but it is not autonomous, and it has thousands of ties with human life and thought. When artists cease to consider the world in its manifold forms outside the artistic domain, their art withers into nothingness, because it no longer has anything to say.

Much abstract art today is art, yes; but it has little meaning because it is only art. All its ties with reality have been cut. This applies as much to a ceramic product as to a painting. Art has its own meaning and needs no excuse. But it loses its meaning if it does not want to become anything but art and therefore cuts its ties with life and reality, just as scholarly work loses its importance and interest if learning is sought for its own sake. Art and science become aestheticism and scholasticism if made autonomous. They become meaningless idols.

The artist's work can have meaning for the society God put him in if he does not go to live in the ivory tower, or try to play the prophet or priest, or—turning in the other direction—in false modesty consider himself only a craftsman. He has to make art while thinking of his neighbors in love, helping them, and using his talents in their behalf.

5. Most art today expresses a spirit, the spirit of our age, which is not Christian. In some ways it is post-Christian, in others anti-Christian, in still others humanistic. Here and there are Christian artists themselves who try to do their work in a godly spirit. But often their brethren leave them alone, distrusting their creativeness or doubting that they are Christians. False art theories that have pervaded the Christian world— the artist as an asocial being, a nonconformist in the wrong sense, a dangerous prophet, an abnormal being who lives in an alien world—are often responsible for this attitude. But some Christian artists themselves hold these false views and look down with contempt at their fellow Christians. Anyway, there is a lot of confusion.

That the art of the world at large is also in a deep crisis does not make things easier. We live in a society where there is a break manifest between the mass of men and the elite, and another break between the natural sciences and technical realities on one side and religion (most of the time rather mystical) of a completely subjectivistic and irrationalistic type on the other. We who live in this world cannot act as if these deep problems did not exist.

There is no real Christian tradition in the arts today to turn to. If an artist wants to work as a Christian and do something he can stand for and bear responsibility for, he has to start with the freedom based in a true faith in the living God of Scripture. He has to make art that is relevant to our day. Therefore, he has to understand our day. And, in order to gain from all that is good and fine today and yet avoid being caught by the spirit of our age and its false art principles, he must study modern art in all its different aspects deeply and widely. He must try to analyze the language modern artists use, their syntax and grammar, in order to be able to hear correctly the message they profess to speak. To analyze, understand, and criticize lovingly, loving man but hating sin, in order to avoid their mistakes but gain from their achievements—that is the Christian artist's task. A new Christian tradition, as a fruit of faith, can only grow if artists who understand their work and task, their world and its problems, really set to work.

6. But what has the Christian artist to offer to the world? He has a freedom to do something, not just the freedom for freedom's sake. What should he aim at? Let's be careful not to lay down new rules. There are no biblical laws that art must be realistic or symbolic or sentimental, or must seek only idealized beauty.

The artist as a Christian is free, but not with a purposeless freedom. He is free in order to praise God and love his neighbors.

These are the basic laws. What do they mean in practice? May I refer, this time without comment, to Philippians 4:8—"Finally, brethren, whatsoever things are true, whatsoever things are honest, whatsoever things are just, whatsoever things are pure, whatsoever things are lovely, whatsoever things are of good report; if there be any virtue, and if there be any praise, think on these things." Here we read what a Christian standing in freedom as a new man, in God's strength and with the help of the Holy Spirit, must search for. This also applies to the Christian as an artist. It is up to him to work, to pray, and to study, in order that he may realize as much as he possibly can of these truly human and life-promoting principles.

In the Lord,

H. R. ROOKMAAKER
Diemen, The Netherlands
August 23, 1966
(used by permission of Christianity Today)

Calvin Seerveld

Until I read *Rainbows for a Fallen World* by Calvin Seerveld, I did not know it was possible to articulate what were to me only the vague feelings and intuitions I had had about creativity and faith. That insightful and creative work opened a door for me that led to the writing of this book. Seerveld writes and lectures with an artistic knowledge and infectious joy. He shatters the idolizing of the arts in his books and presents the biblical truth that art is a call to worship. He is the founder and senior member emeritus in philosophical aesthetics at the Institute of Christian Studies in Toronto, and he lectures all over the world.

Dear young artist,

Let me be as practical as Christ, who said we are to love God above all and love the neighbor as we respect ourselves (Matthew 22:31-39). The Bible tells us further that if we bear the burdens of our neighbor we will be fulfilling the law of Christ (Galatians 5:25—6:2).

This word of God for us as artists is not any easier than it is for a politician or an economist in our complicated, secularized day. But this biblical injunction is a guideline for blessing, because it extricates you from the moil of serving yourself, of doing what is right or just in your own eyes and from thinking you need to jump into the swim of whatever elite or pop art scene is current.

I could put what I believe is wise counsel for those who would be artists in God's world another way. Make your paintings, poetry, sculptures, songs, photography, stories, theatre pieces, music, or whatever artistry: craft it as a psalm before the face and ear of the Lord and let your neighbor listen in. Join the progeny of David, Asaph, Bezalel and Oholiab (Exodus 31:1-11), even the descendants of Korah (Psalms 42—49), and make merry before the Lord God, God's people, and even one's antagonists (Psalm 23:5). Also be as free as the biblical psalmists to cry out to God from the pits of despair in your need, to stop the persecution,

Lord, suffered by Christ's followers nearby or faraway (Psalms 69; 109; 137). And make these psalms for settings outside the worshiping church door. Let them be heard on the radio, appear in art galleries, come across the boards in a theatre and be printed in books.

To become an artist means you become a professional imaginator in order to help your handicapped, unimaginative neighbor. Our artistic profession is meant to give voice, eyes, ears and tactile sense to those who are underdeveloped toward such rich nuances of meaning in God's creation.

Only God could make a tree and fashion a walrus, conceive precious stones that glint mysteriously in the dark depths of the earth. Only God could grace the loving, awkward union of faithful erotic intimacy between a man and a woman with such satisfying pleasure, and provide the hug of a family, schooling, neighborhoods and country for us humans to thrive within.

But artists have the calling to make such treasures known to those who walk past such creatural riches without experiencing them. We artists disclose such creational blessings by fashioning a necklace of words (a poem) or the jewel of a melody (a song) for our neighbor about these great deeds of the Lord.

A Christian artist should also treat sin as the Bible does and not look the other way as the Pharisees did (Luke 10:25-37). But it will be important for you and me not to be self-righteous when we as Christian artists treat evil. The waste that sin brings into God's good world and the addiction of us sinners who can't break out of the habit of being deceptive, smug or violent should bring sadness into the theatre pieces we write, not angry coldness. Sorrow must define our sculptures about war rather than let them become monuments to idealized heroics.

Because respectable-looking church-goers often have terrible problems in the hidden recesses of their lives, I think we need "lament teams" along with the trend for "praise choruses." Artists need to serve their neighbor who is hurting with more than escape and must weep in art with those who are weeping (Romans 12:14-15). To write elegies, memorials and sad songs that are authentic, we as artists will need to crawl compassionately inside the very skin of those who are starving, displaced, depressed, victimized, fanatic with hatred, so the grace we artistically bring is not cheap.

Maybe September 11, 2001, can give us North Americans new horizons for understanding the suffering that has been going on, and is immense and poignant right now as you read this letter, throughout God's world far from our shores, where real people are being slowly terrorized by famine and cruelty. We Christians have neighbors and enemies, and we know what the Lord requires: art that cries out at our sin and promises the mercy of the Lord for those who plead for help (Micah 6:6-8; Luke 6:17-38).

I assume you will train to become a skilled artisan in the art of your choice (Psalm 33:3). You do not have to aspire to be a "star" in the eyes of world society, like a comet shooting across the media sky. If you are faithful in providing nuanced manna in small venues, the Lord will prepare you for service in larger settings (Matthew 25:14-30).

The key thing is to be a reliable artist in the imaginative task you perform. God loves amateur artists too, if they do not show off. But the Lord asks each one of us to hone our gifts with disciplined respect for the task at hand so the fruit of our imaginative hands can be wholesome food for those who receive it. Find a talented mentor in your art form whom you can trust, and become a craftsmith worthy of hire.

Your redemptive task as artist is not to convert people or to be apologetic about following Jesus Christ. A Christian artist simply needs to give away your imaginative insights to whoever crosses your path, and the Holy Spirit will take it from there.

And when a disbeliever in the Christ experiences in your short story a wrestling with God as Jacob did with the angel (Genesis 32:22-32) or as the poetic author of Psalm 39 did with the Lord God self; or if a stranger is caught by your painting and finds your trusting in God (as in Alan Paton's novels) to be winsome; or if your song of passionate love for a friend through thick and thin sounds unusual to a hard-hearted listener, making the listener jealous (as Paul says in Romans 11:13-14) for love that lasts beyond a sensual four-letter trick, then you as artist have been a faithful imaginative trustee of God's gift to you (Matthew 24:36-51).

It is always important for us as artists not to be so heavenly minded that we are no earthly good, but to be earthy with our redemptive cheer, down in the muck of life too, so that the imaginative grit we offer gives the resilience of hope to the neighbors who are dispirited.

The Holy Spirit is the true source of the wisdom an artist needs to find his or her long-range place in society. Because artistry in Western culture has been either wrongly estranged from ordinary working life or has often been forced to become commercialized and formulaic to be acceptable by the masses, young artists with integrity have often needed to find non-artistic work related to their art in order to put bread on the kitchen table.

Christian artists have a responsibility to help overcome this sense of artistic alienation and displacement in society by making their art speak for neighbors. Give the neighbors what they imaginatively need, not just what they want, and wait patiently upon the Lord for blessing.

A good artistic photograph or song about human love and about human tragedy that breathes a sense of God's hovering presence, which bespeaks obliquely that God's got the whole damaged world in God's hands, is a worthy living sacrifice of obedience in response to Christ's command, "Follow me, young artists."

Artists have the glorious calling to intercede imaginatively for others, to increase perseverance and dispense a simple joy and peace that surpasses understanding (Philippians 4:4-7).

A good way not to feel lonely as an artist who would serve the Lord in deed is to realize you are a member of a community. You must not pity yourself as Elijah did and think you are the only displaced artist left faithful to the Lord (1 Kings 19:1-8). You are not only a member of a church community—which sometimes has little place for artists unless they do "church art"—but a person in the numberless throng and communion of artistic saints who have existed since Adam's poem for Eve before our fall into sin (Genesis 2:23).

So go find an example of Christian artistry in history—Ravenna mosaics, Reformation portraiture, German chorales, Puritan diaries, Russian novels, Afro-American rural blues or gospel, or any particular person in your art form who breathes the mind of Christ—distill their *contribution in disciplined fashion, update it, make it new through your own lived history, and then throw it like bread out upon the waters around you. God helping you it will not get lost but bring healing sustenance to those who are hungry and thirsty (Ecclesiastes 11:1-6).*

No matter how difficult your own life may become as an artist, those who give away their artistry for the imaginative support of their neighbor, as an obedient thank you to the Lord, will be given the staying power of shalom until the Lord returns in glory. I pray that the church of Jesus Christ will grow the vision to support you in this preparation for the rule of the Lord God over all aspects of his world which is coming.

May God rest you merry at times, weary one. God keeps all your tears in God's bottle (Psalm 56:8).

CALVIN SEERVELD
Toronto, November 2001

Nicolae Moldoveanu

I met Nicolae Moldoveanu on a recent tour of Romania. He had been sentenced to twelve years at hard labor by the Communist dictator Nicolae Ceausescu for writing Christian music. During his time of imprisonment (he was finally released because officials feared he would die as a result of the severe beatings he had received in prison), having been denied paper and pen, he would spread soap film on the window of his cell and write music with his finger on the glass. After he was finished he would commit the piece to memory. Upon his release he wrote down over three hundred songs from memory! The man I met, though advanced in years, was cheerful and full of the Spirit. His wisdom does not come from scholarly deliberation as much as from suffering. The following letter is a translation from Romanian.

My dear fellow artist,

There are always two perspectives when we want to make an evaluation. One is the divine perspective—when everything is considered from God's point of view; the other is the human perspective—when everything is considered from our point of view. When we see things from our perspective we make mistakes. But when we evaluate something taking into consideration God's perspective described in the Word of God we cannot fail. This is what we have to do when we talk about Christian artists or Christian music.

Any Christian artist is—first of all—a Christian, a child of God, and then an artist. And a Christian is a new creation in Jesus Christ. There is a whole new perspective and a whole new set of values in his life.

Christian art, whether it be painting, poetry, or music, is an essential part of the authentic Christian life. We need to consider it in the context of a life that has the person of Jesus Christ as a role model. The Lord is revealed and His presence is made real to us through music. Music is the gift God gave His believers for praise and worship. There are two gifts from God that will remain with us in the life to come—love and music. God created this earth in the sound of music, and we could say that the whole Universe has been created in the sound of music. God told Job, "Where were you when I laid the earth's foundation? Tell me, if you understand. Who marked off its dimensions? Surely you know! Who stretched a measuring line across it? On what were its footings set, or who laid its cornerstone—while the morning stars sang together and all the angels shouted for joy?" (Job 38:4-7, NIV).

The spiritual song prepares the soul for the work of the Spirit of God in the human heart. Our main concern—as Christian artists—should be to reflect the character of the Lord in the music we sing. Music has the power to poison or to heal one's soul. The truly divine inspired song comes out of the lips that God opened. The prerequisite for a person who wants to praise God through singing, and to serve Him wholeheartedly through music is for that person to be gathered from the vanishing that the sin produced in his or her life. In order to sing to the Lord you must be light in every aspect of your life, in every corner of your innermost being. Darkness is the enemy of the Christian musician because it is the enemy of God. If the comfort of God in someone else's life is the result of our singing, we must go on singing. If not, we should keep silent.

As long as we keep something from our lives for ourselves, we will have obstacles to overcome in serving the Lord, and our singing will be out of tune. When we yield to God everything we are and everything we have, when we no longer pursue the satisfaction of our ego, when the praise of the Lord and of His work becomes our goal, only then we can truly sing to God.

I think that Christian music should prepare the soul for prayer and *the way to the Savior. The Christian artist does not make art for the sake of the art, nor does he sing for the sake of the singing. He proclaims the Gospel for the lost, and He praises God and worships Him by his singing. St. John Chrisostom said, "The person who knows how to sing praises to the Lord will never boast." The music that the world loves, the rhythms of the world transform the heart to a bar, not to the holy temple of God. This kind of music becomes a drug for those who listen to it because it dulls the senses of the listener. Christian or evangelical music prepares the way for the coming of the Holy Spirit in the human heart (cf., 2 Kings 3:15). The soul that has the harp of the heart tuned daily by the Great Master Musician—the Lord Jesus—has all that is needed for singing the music of the Lord.*

Christian musicians should make songs that speak about what Jesus Christ has done in their lives. If Christian artists walk under the guidance of the Holy Spirit, they will not fail. They will have discernment and they will know what comes from God and what comes from the world of this age. In the ancient times, the people of God—the people of Israel—did not have two kinds of music. They only knew music to worship God. Neither do the people of God, those under the New Covenant, His Church, have two kinds of music, two kinds of speaking or two kinds of serving, but only one for the glory of God. Christian music should move our heart for worship, and not our feet for dancing. May the Lord help us to understand this truth and may His work advance through all those who preach, sing, write and serve for the glory of God.

Let us not forget that our song is nothing but an echo, an imitation of the angels' song. Music was created in heaven. Around and above us there are angels singing. If man sings, it is because of a revelation of the Spirit of God. The singer is inspired by God. And while it may be true that music could be studied as a science, it is also art. And this form of art should draw us closer to God. St. Augustine said that through music we could listen fully to the hidden harmonies of the Scripture.

NICOLAE MOLDOVEANU
Sibiu, Romania, August 3, 2001

Chapter Eleven

THE GREATEST EXPRESSION OF CREATIVITY

The Giving of the Self

*I*n a matter of moments he would be arrested. In a matter of hours he would be dead. Yet we do not see Jesus cowering or hiding, and, though he is certainly sad, he does not seem worried. He comes to Bethany—about twenty minutes' walk from Jerusalem, or Gethsemane, or Golgotha—to the home of a man we know only as Simon the leper. His nickname implies that though he might have once been leprous, he had almost certainly been a beneficiary of Jesus' healing ministry.

No one noticed the woman at first. She had slipped in by a side entrance. In the middle of the meal she tiptoed to the place behind Jesus, who was reclining on his left elbow, Roman style. There she lingered for a moment . . . and then from the folds of her gown she produced a white alabaster jar. Moving to his side, without saying a word, she began to slowly pour the costly perfumed oil on his head. It ran down his forehead, dripping from both his eyebrows, wetting his lips and finally disappearing into his beard.

It was creative. It was unexpected. It was irritating. The disciples were angry at what seemed a great waste, a year's wages poured out in the dust. They could have done something practical with the money, like feed the poor (as if such a tenderhearted and generous woman would have ever neglected the poor).

What the nameless woman did that unforgettable evening created a space in time, a space where the disciples could hear God— or not. But Jesus was the only person listening to the loving silence of what she had done. As they began to voice their disapproval, Jesus became indignant. "Leave her alone!" he said, wiping the perfume from his eyes. And then he spoke a word he seldom used, a word that is absolutely central to our understanding of what creativity and art and the imagination are all about. "Beautiful," he said. "What she has done to me is beautiful."

THE TRUE GIFT

Jesus makes a completely unique pronouncement over the nameless woman. This is the only record we have of his saying anything remotely like it. "Wherever the gospel is preached throughout the world, what she has done will also be told, in memory of her." It is not the woman who is memorialized; it is what she did. But because of what she did, she will never be forgotten. And what did she do?

She gave him something—something infinitely more valuable

than the perfume. She found a creative, imaginative way to give herself, to let Jesus know that he was loved and that he was not completely alone in being misunderstood—that is, there was at least one other person who had heard what he said about dying soon. She had come to demonstrate her love while she could. And we will never forget her for it.

Like the woman, we have more to give than gifts. The greatest, most beautiful expression of our creativity is to find a way to give ourselves.

Certainly Jesus had wonderful gifts to give: miracles, bread, wine and, perhaps most significant, healing. That seemed to be the main reason the crowds hounded him. And he patiently, though sometimes reluctantly, doled out these gifts to them, to thousands of them! But if you look more closly at his life and listen to the Gospels, you get the distinct impression there was more he was after. More that he wanted to give. Jesus had a habit of pursuing people in order to give them more.

In John 5 we encounter a bizarre little man I call the "man of excuses." For thirty-eight years this wretched little geek has been lounging beside the pool of Bethesda, pitifully clinging to his most treasured possession, his illness.

Now Jesus finds the man and loves him enough to ask a seemingly ludicrous but piercing question, "Do you want to get well?"

The man begins to rehearse the list of excuses he has been reciting since he was a boy. "No one will help me," he whines. "Someone always pushes in front of me."

Despite the man's whining, his lack of courage to become well and his faithlessness, Jesus utters the command, "Get up." Apparently the only thing that was left for the man to do was to get up, pick up his mat and walk. And that's all he does. There is no mention of his giving thanks for being healed. We do not hear him beg to become a follower, like the man from the tombs. The little coward simply walks away, not even learning the name of the One who healed his lame legs. Apparently his legs were all Jesus chose to heal that day, because the man's heart seems to have remained untouched.

When the Jews object to the man's carrying his mat on the sabbath, breaking their oral law, the man turns, points a bony finger in the direction of the crowd and snivels, "He told me to do it." Only Jesus has slipped away through the crowd. And that was the miracle. Or was it?

What happens next tells us more about the heart of Jesus than the miracle of his healing power. John tells us that Jesus found the man. He went looking for him in the crowd and discovered that he was in the temple area.

"Stop sinning or something worse will happen to you," Jesus says.

Something worse? Something worse than be crippled for almost forty years? Yes, something infinitely worse: meeting Jesus and not coming to really know him.

You see, Jesus has given the man a gift, healing. But Jesus is more than his gifts. He wants to give the man more. He wants to give him himself.

GIFTS AND THE GIFT

If this were the only incident of Jesus seeking someone after he had healed them it might be different, but the Gospels are filled with such stories. In John 9 we read about the man who was born blind. Jesus places mud on his eyes and sends him away to experience the healing in Jesus' absence. Though Jesus has given him the gift of sight, the man does not know what Jesus looks like or what his name is.

Once again the Jews object to the kindness of Jesus. They do not have eyes to see the miracle of a person's sight restored. They only see the infraction of one of their rules. (Jesus spit to make the mud, and it was against their law to spit on the sabbath!)

Again, after a somewhat humorous investigation, Jesus looks for and finds the man. The drama of the moment is awesome.

"Do you believe in the Son of Man?" Jesus asks.

"Who is he, sir?" the man replies.

"You are looking at him," says Jesus.

What an enormous gift had been given to the man that morning. To see for the first time in his life! But how much greater was the gift he received after Jesus looked for and found him. Are you beginning to see it for yourself? Jesus is not his gifts. He longs to give us more. He wants to give us himself!

We could talk about the woman with the bleeding problem, whom Jesus sought out in the midst of the throng. He wanted her to have more than the healing that restored her life; he wanted her to have himself (Luke 8:40).

We could talk about the woman at the well in John 4. Once again, Jesus offered himself to her, but because her soul was so dead she mistook Living Water for well water. She almost missed it, but Jesus pursued her. We could talk about Zacchaeus (Luke 19) whom Jesus found in—of all places—the top of a tree. We could look at any of the postresurrection experiences and see the same thing. Jesus, having already given all he could, seeks out men and women to see them again, to touch them and be touched by them.

WHAT ABOUT US?

Gifts are wondrous things. They can heal and feed people, and even set them free. We sometimes spend enormous amounts of time and money strengthening and developing them, and there is nothing wrong with that. The process of giving a gift to someone, whether it is a poem for a friend or a huge exhibit that tours the world, is a thrilling experience for everyone involved. But don't settle for that.

We are called to give more. If Jesus is truly our paradigm and pattern, as we confess he is, then like him we must constantly be searching for new and creative ways to give ourselves to others for his sake. That is true creativity. It does not require perfect pitch. It does not demand digital dexterity. In fact, it does not demand anything at all—except surrender. This is not to say that it is easy. There is a level of giving that we can achieve only through brokenness, but the burden is light precisely because the One who places it on our lives never completely takes his hand from under the weight. He never stops pursuing us, even to the very last moment of our lives. He creates a space in time that allows us to hear, understand and respond to his extravagant invitation. He welcomes our creative, worshipful response. He promises to never leave or forsake us, to never stop tracing his pattern in the sacred soil that is our lives.

I want to leave you where we started, in the temple court. It is still a chilly morning. The first silence of the scribbling has come and gone. Jesus has spoken his authoritative word. Now he has returned to the sand, on his knees with his feet out behind him. His tongue is still sticking out from the corner of his mouth. Can you hear it now? The silent, taut tension, the frame around those ten words. It leaves us standing, gaping with the angry mob, watching him on his knees, the content of his writing unknown and unknowable.

In that holy, irritating moment, some of us drop the cruel stones we have been clutching, realizing there is no place here for that kind of anger. Some then wander off, unchanged, having heard nothing in the silence of the moment but the scratching of his scribbling.

But, by grace, a few of us get down on our knees and join Jesus in the childlike, playful moment. In our differing moments lights come on and go off inside our souls. It is a timeless moment. There is something wordless about it, and yet it is so full of meaning.

There is, as there always will be, a dull, gray group standing around us protesting our waste of time and talent. But more important, there are those who are "getting it"—whose imaginations are being recaptured by the moment, who have begun to sense inside themselves a hunger being fed. These few have begun to realize that our world is not the only world that exists. All this and infinitely more, occurring all at once in time—hearing, listening, feeling, understanding. And all the while, we scribble in the sand.

GROWING IN CREATIVITY

Some Practical Advice

everal friends, upon reading the manuscript of this book, said that I needed to include some practical advice. For their sake, here, reluctantly, are a few important ideas.

1. Allow the Bible to speak for itself. Develop a listening stance to Scripture, no matter how shocking or risky the message might be.

2. Always point to Christ and away from yourself (avoid the personal pronoun at all costs). Allow yourself to become "hidden in Christ" (Colossians 3:3).

3. Never allow the vehicle to overpower the message. The vehicle must be appropriate to the message. It must reflect an interdependence with the message.

4. Risk not being understood; risk not saying everything all the time.

5. The Bible calls forth the fullest range of human emotion, from anger and disappointment to praise and worship. Therefore, be honest.

6. Do all that you can do to be a part of, foster, and pour yourself into community. Do your best to make that community a part of your own fellowship. If nothing like that exists in your church, seek to establish one. If that is not possible, put together a local group that is composed of believers. It can be evangelistic in character—not absolutely closed to nonbelievers—but care should be taken, for problems can quickly and subtly arise when a different value system is introduced into your group.

7. Share with your community the things you create, for all the obvious reasons.

8. Seek to further your understanding of humility, servanthood and radical obedience as they relate to your craft. Allow the things you learn there to pervade every area of your life.

9. Remember that creativity can be seasonal. There can be springtime surges of creative energy. There can also be winter times of frustrating cold.

10. Remember that one of the greatest freedoms you possess is the freedom to fail. We are not called to succeed all the time. We are called to be faithful to the call of Christ on our lives.

11. Never cease praying that you will not become a star or celebrity. Donald Davidson has said, "Our culture places an absolute premium upon various kinds of stardom. This degrades and impoverishes ordinary life, ordinary work, ordinary experience."

Bibliography

Bass, Alice. *The Creative Life*. Downers Grove, Ill.: InterVarsity Press, 2001.

Bausch, William. *Storytelling: Imagination and Faith*. Mystic, Conn.: Twenty-Third Publications, 1984.

Bayles, David and Ted Orland. *Art and Fear*. Santa Barbara, Calif.: Capra Press, 1993.

Berry, Wendell. *Standing by Words*. San Francisco: North Point Press, 1983.

_____. *Life is a Miracle*. Washington: Counterpoint Press, 2000.

Best, Harold. *Music Through the Eyes of Faith*. San Francisco: Harper Collins, 1993.

Boorstin, Daniel. *The Creators*. New York: Random House, 1992.

Bryant, David. *Faith and the Play of the Imagination*. Macon, Ga: Mercer, 1989.

Cameron, Julia. *The Vein of Gold*. New York: Putnam, 1996.

Chaplin, Adrienne and Hilary Brand. *Art and Soul*. Downers Grove, Ill.: InterVarsity Press, 1999.

Charlotte, Susan. *Creativity*. Troy, Mich.: Momentum Books, 1993.

Coles, Robert. *The Call of Stories*. Boston: Houghton Mifflin, 1989.

Copland, Aaron. *Music and the Imagination*. Cambridge: Harvard University Press, 1952.

Davenport, Guy. *The Geography of the Imagination*. New York: Pantheon, 1954.

Davidson, Donald. *I'll Take My Stand: The South and the Agrarian Tradition by 12 Southerners*. New York: Harper TorchBooks, 1930.

Dillard, Annie. *The Writing Life*. New York: HarperPerennial, 1989.

Eliade, Mircea. *Symbolism, the Sacred, and the Arts.* New York: Continuum, 1992.

Elsheimer, Janice. *The Creative Call.* Colorado Springs: Shaw, 2001.

Erickson, Kathleen. *At Eternity's Gate: The Spiritual Vision of Vincent van Gogh.* Grand Rapids, Mich.: Eerdmans, 1998.

Forbes, Cheryl. *Imagination.* Portland, Ore.: Multnomah Press, 1986.

Gaebelein, Frank. *The Christian, the Arts, and the Truth.* Portland, Ore.: Multnomah Press, 1973.

Gardner, Howard. *Creating Minds.* New York: Basic Books, 1993.

Goleman, Daniel, *The Creative Spirit.* New York: Plume, 1992.

Heschel, Abraham. *I Asked for Wonder.* New York: Crossroad, 1983.

Holmes, Arthur. *The Making of a Christian Mind.* Downers Grove, Ill.: InterVarsity Press, 1985.

L'Engle, Madeleine. *Walking On Water.* Colorado Springs: Waterbrook Press, 1980.

Maisel, Eric. *Fearless Creating.* New York: Putnam, 1995.

Marshall, Paul with Lela Gilbert. *Heaven Is Not My Home.* Nashville: Word, 1998.

Nelson, Victoria. *On Writer's Block.* Boston: Houghton Mifflin, 1993.

Nisenson, Eric. *Ascension: John Coltrane and His Quest.* New York: Da Capo Press, 1995.

Noland, Rory. *The Heart of the Artist.* Grand Rapids, Mich.: Zondervan, 1999.

O'Conner, Flannery. *Mystery and Manners.* New York: Noonday Press, 1957.

Prior, David. *Creating Community.* Colorado Spring: NavPress, 1992.

Rilke, Rainer Maria. *Selected Poems of Rainer Maria Rilke*. New York: Harper and Row, 1981.

Rookmaaker, H. R. *The Creative Gift*. Westchester, Ill.: Cornerstone Books, 1981.

Ryken, Leland. *The Liberated Imagination*. Wheaton, Ill.: Harold Shaw Publishers, 1989.

_____. *The Christian Imagination*. Grand Rapids, Mich.: Baker, 1981.

Sacks, Oliver. *Seeing Voices*. San Francisco: Harper Collins, 1989.

Sawyer, Joy. *Dancing to the Heartbeat of Redemption*. Downers Grove, Ill.: InterVarsity Press, 2000.

Sayers, Dorothy. *The Mind of the Maker*. London: Mowbray, 1941..

Seerveld, Calvin. *A Christian Critique of Art and Literature*. Toronto: Tuppence Press, 1995.

_____. *Rainbows for the Fallen World*. Toronto: Tuppence Press, 1980.

_____. *Bearing Fresh Olive Leaves*. Toronto: Tuppence Press, 2000.

Turner, Steve. *Imagine: A Vision for Christians in the Arts*. Downers Grove, Ill.: InterVarsity Press, 2001.

Veith, Gene Edward. *State of the Arts: From Bezalel to Mapplethorpe*. Wheaton, Ill.: Crossway, 1991.

_____. *Postmodern Times*. Wheaton, Ill.: Crossway, 1994.

Westermeyer, Paul. *Te Deum: The Church and Music*. Minneapolis: Fortress Press, 1998.

Zuidervaart, Lambert (ed). *Pledges of Jubilee*. Grand Rapids, Mich.: Eerdmans, 1995.

About the Author

Michael Card is an award-winning musician, performing artist
and writer of many popular songs, including the classics
"El Shaddai" and "Immanuel."
He has produced over twenty albums, including his latest release,
Scribbling in the Sand: The Best of Michael Card Live.
He is also the author of numerous books,
including *A Violent Grace* and *The Parable of Joy.*
Collectively, his works have sold more than four million copies.

Card has been a mentor to many younger artists and musicians,
teaching courses on the creative process and calling
the Christian recording industry to deeper discipleship.
He lives in Tennessee with his wife and four children.

Card received an undergraduate degree in biblical studies from
Western Kentucky University in 1979. He also had an assistantship,
and taught physics and astronomy in a masters program at WKU.
Michael went on to receive a master's degree in biblical studies from WKU
in 1980. He is currently working on his doctorate in classical literature.

In cooperation with The Bible League, Michael Card has launched the
Michael Card Share the Word Project to provide Bibles to persecuted Christians
and searching people. For over ten years Card has partnered with The Bible
League's efforts to supply Bibles to people around the world.
For more information, contact the Michael Card Share the Word Project,
c/o Bible League, P.O. Box 28000, Chicago, IL 60628, or e-mail
<info@bibleleague.org> or visit <www.michaelcard.com/sponsor.asp>.

Also available from
InterVarsity Press

Scribbling in the Sand Study Guide
8 studies for individuals or groups. 80 pages, paper, 0-8308-2059-0, $5.99.

Scribbling in the Sand Audio Book
Read by Michael Card, includes exclusive interviews and extra material not
available in the book. 2 60-minute CDs, 0-8308-2303-4, $19.99.

For more information about *Scribbling in the Sand*
and its related products, visit:
www.scribblinginthesand.com

For more information about the
ministry and music of Michael Card, contact:

The Card Group
615-790-7675
cardmusci@aol.com
www.michaelcard.com